D1417495

The Business Owner's Basic Toolkit for Success

Joan Hartley

BookPartners, Inc.
Wilsonville, Oregon

The Business Owner's
Basic Toolkit for Success

Joan Hartley

Dedication

Dedicated to my parents, incredibly fine role models
who taught me to be honest, hard working and generous,
and who always nurtured and championed my efforts.
I wish Daddy could have read this book.
I think he would have liked it.

Table of Contents

Part I
Is Business Ownership/
Self-Employment For Me?

1   Clarify Your Personal Values and Establish Goals . .13
2   Inventory Your Personal Attribute 31
3   Conduct a Feasibility Study 51
4   Assess the Risk 65
5   Formalize Your Vision and Mission 81

Part II
How to Build a Successful, Enduring Business

6   Write Your Plan for Success 95
7   The Srategic Planning Process (Applicable Forms) . . .123
8   The Work of the Business Owner 129
9   Anything Worth Doing is Worth Doing Intentionally
    and Systematically 147
10   Watch the Bottom Line 169
11   Enlist Help 183
12   You Can Transform Your Dream Into Reality 195
    Business Owner's Basic Reading List 202
    Index 203

Part One

Is Business Ownership/Self-Employment for Me?

1

Clarify Your Personal Values
and Establish Goals

It's a mystery why some folks are lured by the call to entrepreneurship, much like Odysseus was drawn by the ethereal wail of the sirens. Other people never hear the call or find that it has no allure for them. I know from experience that many people who are beckoned to entrepreneurship are ill-equipped for the journey upon which they embark. Like the ancient rover, Odysseus, they find themselves, not in the paradise which lured them, but in a nightmare from which they may not emerge unscathed. The latest statistics from the Small Business Administration confirm that the rate of closure for businesses remains alarmingly high. It's alarming because there is a human story that accompanies every business failure. Often that story tells of the unnecessary loss of personal savings, bankruptcy, shame, the breakup of a marriage, or the alienation of friends.

I insist these losses are unnecessary because if the losers had possessed the tools for assessing the likelihood and personal costs of failure, and found them to be too high, most surely some would have chosen to steer their ship another way. If those who chose the chancy road to business success had first acquired the tools to do the work of the business owner, nearly all would have reached their destination. That's absolutely true! But most of the folks I know who have found business ownership to be loss-ridden and scary did not possess the tools to transform their passion into a reality. Too often the decision to own a business has been an emotional response to that mysterious call.

In the January, 1998 issue of The Costco Connection, the title of Bill Gates' Technology column was "Entrepreneurship Is Not for Everyone." Here is what one of the most extraordinary entrepreneurs of our time said in his column:

"The word entrepreneur used to be reserved for somebody who started his or her own company. These classic entrepreneurs are often innovative risk-takers, but that does not mean that every innovative risk-taker is an entrepreneur or should be.

"While entrepreneurship is frequently glamorized, there are huge disadvantages to starting your own company. For one thing, I've heard that 90 percent or more of all start-up companies fail. There's not much fun in that.

"For another, most people don't like the job once they have it. The glamour wears off but the stress and drudgery do not. When you start a company, there's a huge range of activities you have to perform and problems you have to figure out. You have to spread yourself pretty thin.

"This is quite a contrast to life inside a company, where a talented person can specialize in what he or she does well. It suits most people better than really being an entrepreneur."

Sometimes the summons to be your own boss comes as an alternative to low job satisfaction. "If I owned this business, I would do a better job of it," you say to yourself. Sometimes the call comes from a desire for more direct reward for effort expended. "I do all the work, and she reaps all the profits!" Sometimes the call comes wearing the cloak of innovation. "I have an idea for a better, novel mousetrap." For many reasons the call comes, all of them valid and compelling to the person who is beckoned.

And nowadays, the call comes louder and more persistently because of at least four developments in the business world — home-based businesses, corporate downsizing, franchises, and multi-level marketing:

• The allure of working at home is almost irresistible. No more commutes. No more stiff collars or ties. No more days of endless meetings. It seems too good to be true. And you know what they say about that — if it seems too good to be true, it probably is. Yes, there are some powerful benefits to working in a home office. But there can also be some negative consequences. First, it takes enormous discipline to maintain focus. There are so many distractions: family, pets, telephone and television to name just a few. Second, working at home can bring an overwhelming feeling of isolation. When someone first makes the transition from a busy corporate office to a home office, the quiet seems refreshing. After awhile, though, the home worker discovers that the lack of interruptions removes some of the breaks that help to reduce the intensity of the work. In my own case, I can sit at my computer for four or five hours straight, until I am completely drained and discover I need to hear another human voice and experience the joy of companionship. Third, it is very hard to generate creative brainstorming sessions alone. Some people can be creative when alone, but many others need the stimulation of group interaction.

• It seems like hardly a week goes by that there isn't an article in The Wall Street Journal about another major corporation restructuring and reducing the number of employees by the thousands! Many of the folks who subsequently find themselves out of work are middle-aged, and it can be very difficult to find another corporation interested in hiring a fifty-year-old.

When I worked for an outplacement firm I met many downsized executives who seriously considered business ownership as an option for future employment. They had accumulated years of management experience, and felt it was a natural move from management to business ownership. Fortunately, outplacement firms are well-equipped and well-qualified to help these folks determine their suitability for business ownership. Unfortunately, not all downsized employees are given the benefit of outplacement counseling — many struggle through the process of weighing alternatives of future employment alone. And often, they choose to start or buy a business with little knowledge of how to build a successful company.

• One just needs to pick up most any entrepreneurial publication and turn to the back to find dozens of ads promoting franchise ownership, and while laws prohibit franchisers from making promises about the potential financial return to a franchisee, the ads certainly paint a picture that suggests that with a small investment one can purchase a turnkey operation which will produce a comfortable living for the owner.

Experience indicates reality doesn't always produce this

rosy picture. First, not all franchises are time-tested, successful, turnkey operations. And second, not everyone has the skills and aptitude to run a prosperous business — not even a franchise with an excellent record of success.

Several years ago I encountered a man who owned a printing franchise. He was miserable, not profitable, resigned to losing the investment he had made to purchase the franchise, and he told me he could hardly wait to walk away from the nightmare. Although I did not know him well, I could guess from his demeanor and mannerisms that he lacked to a high degree the attributes that predict success in business ownership.

I have a good personal friend, Candy, who has owned a different franchise in the same printing industry for seven years, and is highly successful in her endeavors. She possesses to a very high degree those predictor attributes. In addition, she has a clear understanding of her personal values, a vision for the future of her business, a stated mission, a dynamic business plan which includes standards against which she measures business performance, and a team of supportive advisors. Also, she has made a commitment to spend time every day doing the work of the business owner.

• A couple of years ago I had occasion to spend two months observing a multi-level marketing business firsthand. Multi-level marketing is a hierarchical apparatus designed to promote wide-scale distribution of a product. The success of each individual in a multi-level marketing structure depends more upon her ability to establish a subordinate level of participants than on her ability to sell a product or service. This becomes increasingly difficult with each ensuing level of participation, because of the inherently finite quality of market share. When I heard the founder of the company talk with a group of struggling second and third level salespeople, it was easy to become mesmerized by the words he used to convey his vision and to believe that it would be easy to attain wealth and comfort. But in reality, as I watched these folks struggle over the course of two months, no one seemed to be gaining wealth or comfort except the first level salesperson. And wow, did she ever possess extraordinary amounts of drive, energy and passion, as well as clearly defined values!

The purpose of this book is not to endorse or criticize franchises or multi-level marketing businesses. There are people who have attained success in both of these types of ventures. I believe, however, that they are no different from any other business endeavor in that their success depends first upon the aptitude of the owner and second upon the owner doing the work of the business owner, not just the work of the business. As Thorstein Veblen wrote in 1923, "business has to do with the intangibles of ownership and only indirectly with the tangible facts of workmanship."

The Work of the Business vs. the Work of the Business Owner

Before embarking upon ownership of any business, it makes sense to thoroughly examine one's personal values and life goals to see if they are consistent with business ownership. In my experiences working with small businesses, I have frequently noticed that many owners find that owning their businesses does not provide them with a sense of fulfillment. And in almost every case that I can recall, these unfulfilled owners are passionate about doing the work of the business and are highly skilled to perform that work, but ill prepared to do the work of the business owner. Let me tell you two stories based on fact, but whose details

I have altered.

Rob was a talented carpenter who worked as a subcontractor in the residential building industry. Eventually, Rob concluded that he could make significantly more money as a general contractor, and he was comfortable with his knowledge of the home building process. He found it impossible to secure bank financing for a start up venture in construction, and he already had a sizable mortgage on his home. However, he was able to negotiate a personal loan, secured by his home, from his best buddy Carl.

For several years Rob worked as a general contractor building modestly priced 'spec' houses, several at a time. He personally did most of the framing and carpentry and paid little attention to the details that business owners attend to in successful ventures. Then he was approached to build a very large, very grand custom home. Undertaking this huge project would tap all of his resources and meant that he could not work on any other houses concurrently. However, he welcomed this opportunity to move into a higher income bracket so he accepted the challenge. Unfortunately, the unthinkable happened. Halfway through construction, his customer declared bankruptcy, leaving Rob with unpaid bills and no resources to complete the job because he had all of his eggs in this one basket.

Next, the really unthinkable occurred. Carl seized Rob's home. The ensuing nightmare included loss of a longtime friendship, bankruptcy, loss of self-esteem, and difficulty in securing work as a subcontractor. Rob had enjoyed great fulfillment when he was working with his hands, building houses. But the important work of the owner — goal setting, planning, strategizing, studying financial statements, creating and documenting procedures — was boring and frustrating to him.

Laura had owned her retail gift shop for several years, but the business was in such disastrous financial condition that she was hanging on by the thinnest of threads. She was creative, clever and passionate about what she did (which did not include business planning and financial management), so she eagerly embraced the possibility that someone could help her acquire the skills to build a successful business. That person turned out to be me. Because her husband would have to loan her the money to pay for business development consulting, we arranged a meeting between the three of us.

I was hardly prepared to handle the situation with which I found myself confronted that evening — I should have been trained as a marriage counselor or divorce attorney. It was easy to instantly perceive from his rigid body, crossed arms and firmly set jaw that Frank was seething inside, and it took little encouragement for the cork to explode from the bottled fury. As the tale of the financial disaster of Laura's business unfolded, I learned that it had spilled over into the world of their personal finances. On one occasion, Laura had gotten into Frank's desk to get his business credit card number and expiration date, and used that information to purchase merchandise for her store. The deviousness of her act was unconscionable, and only exacerbated by her inability to pay the invoice when it came due.

By the time I met with them, the financial condition of Laura's business so threatened Frank that he had gone to the bank, cashed in his CDs at a loss, and was carrying the proceeds (many thousands of dollars) on his person at all times, terrified that her creditors would seize his personal assets. It is not hard to understand why Frank was adamant that he would not loan Laura a cent to save her business.

Like Rob, Laura found the work of her business — displaying and selling lovely gifts, matching her merchandise to the needs of her customers — to be exciting and rewarding. But the work of owning and managing the business gave her no joy. Had Rob and Laura understood the work of ownership early in their careers, and examined their personal values and goals to see if they matched that work, they may have chosen a different course and found great satisfaction.

When you have finished reading this book, you will have a good sense of what the work of the business owner is all about. You may then want to return to this chapter and look again at the things you value, that bring a sense of fulfillment into your life. Are the two compatible? Having a 'yes' answer to that question before you embark upon self-employment will greatly increase your probability for success.

Your Passion Will Align with Your Values

Values are the intrinsically desirable, essential nature of your being. There is no judgment attached to them, no sense of right or wrong. Values are who you are, right now. Values are intangible. If you say that money is a value, I encourage you to look beyond the tangible. What is it that the money will do for you? That is what you value.

Marilynn Preston proved that assessing a situation, gambling on one's instincts and making a positive decision in line with one's values is innate to the human spirit. It is only when we go against our instincts, beliefs and personal values that we lose.

Marilynn first discovered fitness — the subject that would make her famous — at age 30, when "gravity was beginning to take over." She was a journalist for the

Chicago Tribune at the time and started a syndicated column called, "Dr. Jock." That was 17 years ago. The column is still around; it is the longest-running nationally syndicated fitness column in the country.

At the same time that she wrote her fitness column, Preston was the newspaper's full-time TV critic. "I couldn't help but notice, with outrage, the miserable job that commercial television was doing for children." So consumed was she with the idea of improving television for kids that she left the Tribune in 1985 to be on her own and to put herself into a position of eventually doing something for children that involved fitness.

While she made videos, wrote a book on fitness, authored two plays, and co-hosted a weekly public affairs show, in the back of her mind was her unmet challenge. She had a lingering passion about somehow linking her two foremost values — kids and fitness.

Having grown up as a tomboy in the South Shore neighborhood of Chicago, Preston had natural coordination, a father who taught her to throw a ball, and a mother who did not comment on her daughter's unladylike behavior. By the time she had become an adult professional, married, but with no children of her own, she had crystallized her vision into a passion: "All I care about is that kids go from inactivity to activity...Girls who do sports in high school are 92 percent less likely to do drugs and 80 percent less likely to get pregnant...What better proof that sports can provide a safe haven for kids?"

After carefully analyzing the potential in her life, Marilynn melded her two chief interests, television and kids, by creating a children's sports and fitness TV show called Energy Express. It uses a clubhouse format, featuring a revolving group of four real-life kids and MTV-style segments. Interviews include kite flyers, bowling aces, swimming champions and bicycle messengers. The premise is simple: let kids tell their own stories in their own words. Sometimes celebrity athletes visit the clubhouse and talk about discipline, passion for their sports, goal-setting visualizations. "'If you can dream it you can do it.' These are the messages that kids need to hear," Preston says. Her philosophy is paying off in other ways too. Today, the Emmy-winning Energy Express is syndicated in 105 cities across the country.

Marilynn Preston's talent, energy and personal values propelled her to create a product about which she was passionate, in an accessible format, that offers better-quality programming for children. Who says one person can't make a difference?

Clarify Your Personal Values

Clarifying your values is not a decision making process, but a course of discovery. Values clarification is a powerful tool in determining whether or not a given decision will prove to be fulfilling. Once values are clearly delineated, it is possible to create personal goals that are consistent with those values and that will prove to be fulfilling.

Some people find it very easy to list their values. In case you need some help in clarifying yours, here are some suggestions to assist you in your discovery. It is usually helpful to find a quiet, comfortable place where you can relax undisturbed. Have a pad and pencil ready for note taking.

Exercise One: Answer the following questions.
• What must you have in life, beyond the basics of food, shelter, etc.?

- What accomplishments, or measurable events, must occur in your lifetime for you to consider that your life has been satisfying — a life with few, or no, regrets?
- Do you have a secret passion in your life — something that is almost too exciting to actually imagine?
- What do you regard as your role in your community, country, world, and universe?
- If you could devote your life to making a difference in the lives of others, while having resources for the lifestyle you need, would you do it? How would your life look?
- What is missing in your life, that if present, would bring fulfillment to your life?
- Describe your life purpose: what is it? how does it impact your day-to-day living? how do you know it's the right purpose for you?

Exercise Two:

Think back to a time and/or situation in your life when you felt happy, energized, enthusiastic, contented. What were you doing at that time? If possible, use old photographs taken at a time when life was particularly good to trigger your recollection. Make detailed notes about the work you were doing, your physical surroundings, your leisure activities, your family situation, etc.

Exercise Three:

Think back to a time when you were particularly upset or angry. Examine the feelings that caused that anger to discover a value that was being suppressed.

Exercise Four:

Imagine yourself traveling through space to another planet — a planet that is identical to Earth except that it is exactly thirty years ahead of our planet. When you arrive on the planet you find yourself at a house. You go to the door, knock, and are greeted by yourself — the person you will be thirty years from now. You enter the home and sit down with this person for a conversation. What do you imagine this person would tell you about the work that he or she has done in the past thirty years that has been valuable and important? What accomplishments have brought pleasure and fulfillment? Write the message from your future self on your notepad.

Exercise Five:

Imagine that you are in a room where many people are assembled. As you look around the room, you realize that the occasion for the assembly is a memorial service, and as you linger you become aware that the memorial service is in your honor. None of the people can see or hear you, but you can see and hear them clearly. One by one they stand and offer statements about what your accomplishments have meant to them and about the significance of your life. As you hear what they are saying, write down their statements.

Compose a List of Your Personal Values

Review the notes you have made during these exercises. Within them you will find the keys to what brings you satisfaction — your values. See if you can develop a list of fifteen to twenty values. Now prioritize the top ten. Use a zero-to-ten scale to indicate how fully you are honoring each of these values in your life right now.

One final comment on discovering, clarifying and writing

your personal values: If you found this process to be extremely difficult, maybe even impossible to accomplish on your own, there are resources to help you. Professional coaches are trained to assist their clients with this process. You can contact The Coaches Training Institute at (800) 691-6008 for a list of certified personal and professional coaches.

Establish Life Goals

Now it is time to formulate and write personal life goals that are consistent with your values. Write at least one goal for each value that you are not honoring fully right now. It is crucial that you write these goals, because research has proved that people accomplish the things they commit to writing. Have you ever said that you wanted or needed to do something, and then managed to put it off indefinitely? On the other hand, do you find that when you create a written To Do list you manage to check off every item on that list? As John-Roger and Peter McWilliams tell us in Do It! Let's Get Off Our Buts (A Guide to Living Your Dreams), "Your automatic creative mechanism operates in terms of goals and end results. Once you give it a definite goal to achieve, you can depend on its automatic guidance system to take you to that goal much better than you ever could by conscious thought. You supply the goal by thinking in terms of end results. Your automatic mechanism then supplies the means whereby."

I was fortunate to have a powerful model in my life who followed his passion, wrote goals for what he wanted to achieve in his lifetime, and then not only achieved his goals but far exceeded anything he had imagined.

My father, John Hartley, was the model I speak of. He was the middle son in a family that experienced incredible personal loss during the Depression. The loss of their farm left an indelible imprint on him. Surely he understood the words of Scarlett O'Hara — "As God is my witness, I'll never be hungry again." And so he worked hard at everything he did, continually improving his personal position and, in the process, making a better life for his family. He started as a messenger, worked his way up through bookkeeper, sawyer, service station attendant, advertising salesman, policeman, transportation planner for the City of Portland, and sales manager for Pierce Freightlines. Many of these jobs he held while he completed his college education and raised a family of three children. Eventually his upward progress landed him an offer to be general sales manager of Great Southern Truck Lines, headquartered in Jacksonville, Florida — about as far from Portland, Oregon as you could go and still be in the contiguous 48 states.

It just so happened that at this time, my father was approached to purchase life insurance. In his own words he said, "I had met with a long-time friend who had been in the life insurance business for about a year and a half. Irving Enna invited me to have coffee one day when I met him on the street corner. Over coffee, he proceeded to pin me down about how much life insurance I had. I assured him that I had plenty, maybe $3,000 or $4,000 worth. He said he had an idea that he wanted to show me and asked if he could come to our home. That evening we sat in the kitchen and he explained life insurance to me. He was the first man who had ever explained it to me in a way that made any sense. I said to Irving, 'Do you mean that if I put $294 a year into this policy, if I die, you will pay Lucille $10,000 cash?'

"'That's right.'

"'And if I don't want to do it any more at the end of ten years, you'll give me all my money back?'

"He said, 'That's right.'

"I said, 'Why am I saving that $294 in a savings account when I could do that? I'll take it.' I bought $10,000 worth of life insurance."

But my dad got much more than the life insurance policy — he got the fever! He turned down the offer to move his family to Florida, resigned from his job at Pierce Freightlines, and took up the great passion of his life — solving problems for families and making their lives better.

Initially, it was terrifying to my mother. According to my father's autobiography, "She was upset with me, but she was true blue; we had a disagreement over it, but she said 'It is your responsibility to care for this family. I think it is a mistake, but I will back you up.' And she backed me up every inch of the way."

The first few years were lean, but my father's passion was so strong, that he persevered through the early learning years. "I soon found out there was such a thing as a CLU [Chartered Life Underwriters] designation, and I immediately started on the five-year training program. I did that five years of training in three years and I got my CLU designation in 1961, having started the program in 1958 after I had completed my LUTC [Life Underwriters' Training Council] training, which is a prerequisite to studying for the CLU. As you know, I went on to be the president of the Portland Life Underwriters with some 600 members; I was vice-president of the Oregon State Life Underwriters with 1000 members; I was president of the Chartered Life Underwriters of Portland; and in 1974 I received the supreme award in my life — I was selected the first

Chartered Life Underwriter of the Year for the Portland chapter. That was the crowning accomplishment for me, capped by almost ten years of instructing insurance subjects for the industry at Portland State University."

At the time he wrote his autobiography, that award may have been his crowning glory. But he also merited a lifetime membership in the Million Dollar Roundtable, achieved only by the consistently highest producers in the industry. And finally, twelve days before his death, my father received even a loftier tribute from his peers in the Oregon Life Underwriters Association: "The H.G. 'Bud' Horn Award, presented to John L. Hartley CLU ChFC MSFS in recognition of long time service for the life insurance industry, May 8, 1997."

My father's personal value of serving people, combined with his innate gift as a teacher, propelled him to work in an industry about which he was passionate. It took him nearly twenty years to find this natural fit, and once he did he never looked back. He loved what he was doing, and although he labored long hours and long days, I think he never 'worked' another day in his life.

Your Book

Here is the final suggestion before we move on to taking an inventory of your personal attributes. Set up a three-ring binder with eight dividers. This binder will be your personal workbook — the basis for your successful business plan. Label the eight dividers as follows:

Personal values and goals
How will we get there?
Values/Vision/Mission

Who is going to do the work to get us there?
Where are we right now?
How much will it cost to get where we want to go?
Where do we want to go?
Action plans

File your lists of values and personal goals behind the first divider. At any time you may decide to revise these lists — no problem. This is a workbook, designed to be used, revamped and amended.

2

Inventory Your Personal Attributes

If you have heard it, you will know what I mean — the subtle, persistent call to own a business or be self-employed. Imbedded in the invitation are hints of prosperity, flexible time, doing things your way, and reaping the rewards of your hard work. Far less perceptible, sometimes even invisible, are any suggestions of failure. The excitement generated by the prospect of owning a business predisposes us to think much about the glory of victory, and little about the agony of defeat. We spend most of our obligatory research seeking data that will support our desire to own a business, and we tend to ignore or minimize the perils.

Equally as important, our feasibility studies are primarily focused on the external factors that affect the outcome of business ownership. We study economic indicators, potential customers and the competition. Rarely do we begin by thoroughly evaluating our own set of beliefs, values and abilities to determine if they are compatible with the work we will be doing. While it is generally accepted that not everyone has an aptitude for being a surgeon, or pilot, or computer technician, seldom do we acknowledge that successful business owners have distinct personal traits and abilities.

It's a shame, because there are some pretty fair predictors of success in business ownership — certain attitudes, behaviors, temperaments and skills. So before making a step that can significantly impact your life, take time to assess the degree to which you possess these attributes.

One of these attributes, a positive attitude, is frequently touted as the most important predictor of success in most anything one chooses to do, whether in athletics, arts, school, your profession, etc. I am a firm believer that a positive, can-do attitude is a most powerful influence on achievement, and my office walls have become a regular reader board of positive attitude affirmations such as:

Attitude is Everything. (Unknown)
If you believe you can or cannot, you are 100% correct.
(Henry Ford)

I do not believe that any one attribute can stand alone as a predictor of success. For example, it doesn't matter how positive my attitude, or how many hours I spend studying and practicing, I will never be qualified to play on a professional basketball team. I'm not tall enough, I'm not fast enough, and my eye-hand coordination could never make the cut. There is no shame associated with my lack of qualifications and I don't wallow in self-pity because I don't meet the requirements (okay, I'd love to make one of those seven digit salaries). Most of all I refuse to beat myself up attempting to do something I can't.

By taking the time to assess your aptitude for a particular line of endeavor before taking the plunge into business ownership, you may well save yourself hours of distress, the loss of significant amounts of money, and the pain that results from suffering a catastrophe. Taking time means more than just reading through the list of aptitudes favorable to business success shown later in this chapter, and quickly acknowledging the level of each attribute that you possess. Instead, sit down with friends, family, co-workers, and associates in the organizations in which you are active. Ask them to tell you with complete candor how they see you in each of the areas. Let them know you do not need affirmation — you need an honest appraisal because you are considering making a step that could have enormous impact on your future. In business this is called 360-degree feedback — seeking input from people all around us. As much as people normally like to receive positive evaluations, this is the time to seek especially forthright input from people who have worked with you and will hold up a mirror for you to see yourself as others see you. Ask respondents to score your possession of each attribute on a one-to-ten scale (one being low and ten being high), and then to provide as many specific, concrete illustrations as possible about when they have seen you display each attribute.

If you have any concerns that friends and associates might be reluctant to provide candid feedback, you may choose to enlist assistance from a professional coach or career counselor. Together you can create a questionnaire to be submitted to your list of contacts. The contacts submit their responses to the third party with assurance that, while their feedback will be forwarded to you, their identities will remain anonymous.

If you complete your own honest evaluation first, there will probably be no surprises in the responses of your associates. Although they may be able to remind you of some specific occasions when certain attributes were prominent or obscure, their assessment will most likely be a confirmation of what you already know about yourself. But don't let that prospect of affirmation keep you from pursuing thorough 360-degree feedback as part of your due diligence, because you are going to score your possession of each of these attributes on a scale of one to ten, and the more input you receive, the more precisely you can define your place on the scale.

One of the most poignant stories of business failure I have read appeared in the October 1997 issue of Inc. magazine. It tells of the closing of a thirty-four-year-old security system installation company. The details surrounding the closing of the business are distressing. What touched me most, however, were the paragraphs reproduced below, because they provide a peek into the heart and soul of the owner (who, by the way, wrote an article in 1990 for Inc. magazine in which he chronicled the course he took in buying this dream business):

"But the worst part of the seven and a half years was the overwhelming sense of hopelessness, of fearing that I would never, ever be able to dig out of the hole. I hated the business, hated the industry, hated the job. Yet I would not, could not, give up or give in. My house was the ultimate collateral for the loan I'd taken out to buy the business. Therefore, lose the business, lose the house. I was trapped, and I couldn't turn the situation around, either.

"When your company is perpetually in financial trouble, you spend a lot of time apologizing and making excuses for not being able to keep your commitments. That is humiliating. In that kind of pressure cooker, you are easily tempted to get angry, hold a grudge, call someone a well-deserved name, fib, cheat, prevaricate, fudge, exaggerate, and mislead, just to survive. That shows you your character—and sometimes it's not a pretty sight."

Business ownership is an enormously gratifying occupation. But if you don't possess the skills, attributes and tools to perform the job well, the outcome could be a disaster. Do not rush into the commitment; make time to assess your qualifications.

So here we go with a list of predictor attributes. At the end of this chapter is a table which lists each attribute down the left side, and to the right a grid with a one-to-ten scale. Duplicate this table so that you have one copy for each respondent — you should probably have input from six to ten individuals (the more risk you will be assuming, the more individuals you will want to consult).

Ability/willingness to delegate. Delegating means "letting go" of the need to do everything yourself. It requires a genuine belief in the ability of others to set and accomplish goals, accept responsibility for results, and be committed to their work. Employees want to be respected for their contributions. They seek ownership of their functions and accept accountability for their continuous improvement. Consequently, thriving businesses are open and participative. Proficient, effective owners recognize that vested employees may make mistakes, but they learn and grow through the process of trial and error. Proficient owners also know that nurturing and developing the potential of employees expands the creative problem solving capacity of the business.

Ability to self-manage effectively. There are books, tapes and seminars devoted to the topic of time management. Let's face it, time isn't manageable. There are only twenty-four hours in a day, sixty minutes in each hour and sixty seconds in each minute. What can be managed is one's self and how one uses time. Effective personal management allows one to get things done — the opposite of procrastination — and consists, among other things, of allowing ourselves to be present in the moment, not worrying about the past or the future. It also consists of identifying time wasters and creating systems that eliminate or minimize their impact. Some of these time wasters are: crisis management (fire fighting), over-scheduling and the inability to say no, disorganization and paper shuffling, telephone and personal interruptions, and superfluous meetings. Some wise person once said, "the people who complain the most about not having enough time are the people who don't make good use of the time they have." If the following words of Denis Waitley fit, you may recognize that self-management is not one of your strong suits. "Instead of tackling the most important priorities that would make us successful and effective in life, we prefer the path of least resistance and do things simply that will relieve our tension, such as shuffling papers and majoring in minors."

Ability/willingness to negotiate. Good leaders recognize that there are times when parties to a decision will have differing views, and that being a leader involves allowing others to have input in making the decision. People who are convinced that they are right, and insist upon holding their position and persuading others of its correctness, often miss an opportunity to expand their knowledge and their experience base by seeking to understand the other person's position. Negotiating is a give and take process that requires one to listen carefully, understand fully, and only then attempt to discriminate between the essentials and the dispensables. After the distinction is made, it is possible to prioritize the dispensables so that one can determine which of the dispensables to let go of first. "The smartest thing you can do in a negotiation, often, is keep your mouth shut" (Andrew Tobias, My Vast Fortune).

Assertiveness. Assertive people take action. Many know that for years Babe Ruth held the major league record for home runs in a season. Did you know that he also once held the record for strikeouts? We can't hit a home run every time at bat, and lots of times we will strike out. But if we never swing, we have no chance of hitting a home run! The ability to confront issues requires that one overcome any tendency to ignore problems, realizing that closing one's eyes to problems is a quick route to disaster — problems don't disappear! Meeting uncomfortable situations head on, with an inquisitive, non-threatening, non-punitive demeanor allows one to discover all the facts about those situations. It was the famous author of such remarkable books as The Martian Chronicles, Ray Bradbury, who observed: "If we listened to our intellect, we'd never…go into business, because we'd be cynical. Well, that's nonsense. You've got to jump off cliffs all the time and build your wings on the way down."

Commitment. Commitment, like pregnancy, knows two percentages — one hundred and zero. When one is committed to achieving a value or goal, the principle of 'freedom of no choice' emerges. Most people in this country would argue that our most precious privilege is our freedom to choose. However, there is a greater freedom. When a person has established goals that are in complete harmony with personal values and beliefs, and has made a commitment to reaching those goals, that person enjoys the greatest freedom of all, the freedom from having to choose. When a decision is to be made, a crossroads is reached and alternatives are presented. Each alternative is examined in light of the goal. One of the alternatives will be more in accord than the others and the person moves to that alternative with absolute freedom from doubt or conflict — the greatest freedom of all.

Conclusiveness. Having confidence in one's ability to assess situations and then, by reasoning and logical proof, to move forward decisively, allows one to take advantage of windows of opportunity. Business ownership is not a place for the meek. An owner considers options and evaluates possible outcomes, then decides.

Creativity. Creativity blazes the trail for human progress. There is an old saying, "Insanity is doing things the same old way and expecting a different result." Creativity is generating novel and useful ideas for solving a problem, taking advantage of an opportunity or moving one's agenda forward. Business leaders recognize two mandates regarding creativity: one is to nurture their own creative edge; the other is to encourage creativity in those who surround them.

Desire to learn and grow/curiosity. Learning, not knowing, is one of the keys to success. Acquired knowledge has momentary value since knowledge has a short shelf-life these days. However, being eager to discover and seeking to employ a process of continuous enlightenment opens the door to future knowledge, some of which may perfectly fit a need. Letting go of limiting beliefs is crucial to learning. You may have heard that elephant trainers confine a baby calf by chaining one of its legs to the trunk of a sturdy tree.

No matter how hard the baby elephant pulls, it cannot free itself. It grows up accepting this restraint. By the time it is full grown, it accepts this limitation without question, even though the other end of the chain may now be fastened only to a small stake in the ground from which it could easily free itself. People, too, sometimes succumb to the limiting beliefs we once held to be true. As Thoreau observed, many people lead lives of quiet desperation — stuck in dead-end jobs and seeing no conceivable way out. Successful business owners are not crippled by limiting beliefs, but realize that there is a vast wealth of options available for addressing challenges.

Energy/stamina/health. The rewards of success fall to those who work hard, and energy is a controllable variable in determining ability to work hard. High energy, stamina and good health frequently result from living a balanced life, and people who possess them work intensively but not obsessively. As John Kotter observed in an Inc. magazine article, "The energy level required to build an organization is tremendous. I've been at the Harvard Business School for 25 years, and I'm embarrassed to admit that we do almost nothing to help people understand that."

Exuberance. Exhilaration and vivacity result from possessing an intense level of joy that springs forth from seeing unending possibilities in people and in the environment. Exuberance flows from the attitudes of the successful. As Wayne Dyer said to Richard Carlson, "Number one: Don't sweat the small stuff, and Number two: It's all small stuff." Successful people operate from an abundance mode — there's plenty of everything for everyone, so they are not plagued by worries or concerns. Instead, they delight in the gifts of each day. And they meet new challenges with the assurance that if Plan A doesn't work, there's a profusion of alternative plans and there is a lesson to be learned in facing the challenge.

Flexibility. Flexibility depends on the capacity to learn continuously as well as one's comfort with change and growth. Flexibility compels that we ease up and let go of some rigidly held views. It requires a willingness to step away from one's old habits and closely held policies to try on new behaviors. In business it frequently means shifting gears. Plan A doesn't work? Let's try Plan B!

Focus/clarity. We are constantly bombarded with information — the latest, the newest, the quickest, the surest. Some of the information we receive is important, but much of it has no significance for us personally. Having clarity of purpose means being so absolutely sure of one's purpose that it is possible to weed out the information that is not pertinent, and assimilate only that information that is beneficial. It is being able to keep one's sights squarely on the bull's-eye, when all around the target are distractions.

Genuine regard for people. There is a huge difference between having a tolerance for other people, and having a genuine regard for the ability of people to solve problems, create new ideas, and become self-actualized. Leaders are those people who truly believe that no one of us is greater than any other, and that no one of us can accomplish as much as all of us together. They look for the good in other people, knowing they will find what they look for. Leaders are committed to creating an environment in which people can contribute, and learn and grow. If you want to become rich yourself, first you must enrich others.

Good communication ability. The first requirement for good communication is being a good listener. As some wise person noted, people have two ears and one mouth for a good reason — we should probably listen twice as much as we talk. Being present in the moment and respecting the person who is speaking is a priceless and seldom given gift. As Richard Carlson suggests in Don't Sweat the Small Stuff, "Imagine that everyone you know and everyone you meet is perfectly enlightened. That is, everyone except you! The people you meet are all here to teach you something." Successful people champion others and tell them why they like, admire and appreciate what they do. Another essential of good communication is clarity of thought and the ability to convey summary statements.

Life balance. Having balance between the various aspects of one's life is important for the freshness of perspective it contributes. Generally, those who function freely and effectively allow appropriate amounts of time for career, health, money management, romance, relationships, personal growth, and fun or recreation. This balance furnishes a supportive rather than draining environment. Lack of balance results in exerting great amounts of energy with no satisfaction or accomplishment gained. To live a meaningful life, it is important to support our values with our actions. When we live in harmony with our basic values, we can achieve our goals sooner, with less effort and stress and more satisfaction.

Openness/self-disclosure. Successful people are willing to write and publicly announce their values, goals, vision and mission, to their associates and to the general public. They are also willing to admit that they don't have all the answers. They seek the stories of creative, flexible people and allow themselves to be inspired. They recognize that what others have done, they can do also. Successful people recognize that by sharing the big picture and welcoming feedback they increase the participation of those who are also committed to their success. They also understand that people are willing to follow the lead of, and support, someone who is on the level with them.

Optimism. Optimism is the outward manifestation of high hope. Optimists don't allow negative thoughts to overpower their minds. Instead they continually challenge and dispute negative thoughts. Optimists understand how important a positive attitude is in achieving their goals, and even when setbacks occur, they set new incremental goals and set out to achieve them. They focus on and count their pluses, not their minuses. Movie mogul Sam Goldwyn optimistically commented about a film that had been besieged by problems, "It's an impossible situation, but it has possibilities."

Organizational ability. Because of the enormous volume of information with which we are inundated, it is crucial that one be able to sort through it, select that which is essential, and use a system of organizing data. As my wise mother has told me all my life, organization requires that we have "a place for everything and everything in its place." Being organized requires that one be able to think, prepare and plan in advance. During a recent visit with a client, I asked for some financial information. I watched with compassion as my client fumbled in vain through his desk drawers, stacks of paper on the desktop, and bookcases. It was easy to see why his business affairs were topsy-turvy — they were a reflection of his thought processes and his work habits.

Passion. Passion is absolutely required for high levels of creativity. Successful people are carried by an incredible zeal, a purpose bigger than any problem that might occur. That inextinguishable desire empowers them to find a way to accomplish their goals. Abraham Lincoln believed that God had given him a mission to fulfill. Albert Schweitzer gave up a lucrative medical practice to spend his life caring for the natives of Africa. Helen Keller, though blind and deaf, dedicated her life to helping the less fortunate. Benjamin Disraeli, a Jew, became the prime minister of Great Britain during a time of rampant anti-Semitism. "You can have anything you want if you want it desperately enough. You must want it with an inner exuberance that erupts through the skin and joins the energy that created the world," said the extraordinary Sheila Graham.

Perseverance/persistence. Persistence is refusing to give up when one is committed to an outcome. It is shifting to Plan B when Plan A runs aground. One of my favorite stories tells of a young reporter who was interviewing Thomas Edison after hundreds of unsuccessful attempts to invent an incandescent light bulb. The reporter is supposed to have asked Mr. Edison why he didn't give up on his folly, to which Edison replied, "Young man, you don't seem to understand the way the world works. I have just successfully identified hundreds of ways one cannot create an incandescent light bulb." One element of perseverance is recognizing that there are many potential routes to an outcome — if one route leads to a dead end, another route can be followed. "Many of life's failures are people who did not realize how close they were to success when they gave up," said the father of the light bulb.

Personal sense of well-being. Successful people realize that they are valuable just because they "are." They feel comfortable with just being, and while they may enjoy material possessions, they do not need them to make a statement about their own value. They believe in themselves and trust their own inspiration. They are content with themselves and do not depend on others for recognition of their accomplishments. Successful people also contribute to their community, and while they may receive recognition for their contributions, they don't require any acknowledgment of those accomplishments. As George Bernard Shaw said, "I am convinced that my life belongs to the whole community and as long as I live, it is my privilege to do for it whatever I can, for the harder I work the more I live. I rejoice in life for its own sake. Life is no brief candle for me. It is a sort of splendid torch which I got hold of for a moment, and I want to make it burn as brightly as I possibly can before turning it over to future generations."

Problem solving ability. Strategic thinking begets inventiveness and innovation as a method for solving problems. Problem solving is about using the scientific method, a way of thinking that relies on hypothesis generation and testing. It's about asking "what if" and "if...then" questions. It's about thinking of accomplishment of purpose as an experiment. If one experiment fails, it's trying something else. Seen this way, problem solving is both creative and analytic, a process one cycles through continuously, with each new pass learning something new that promotes development of an increasingly better hypothesis. Knowing is not the key to success — learning is!

Resilience. Buoyant people are unflappable, having the ability to bounce back from setbacks. Successful people who are comfortable with their worth do not see setbacks as personal failures. They possess the inner strength that allows them to regroup, re-focus on their goals and develop new strategies for reaching those goals. They approach life's changes as challenges, and are likely to transform events to their advantage. Less hardy people are more likely to try to deny their setbacks, even to escape them by watching more television, drinking, resorting to drugs or sleeping excessively. Resilient individuals hold these thoughts: I am not defeated. I am lucky. I take advantage of available opportunities. No one is perfect. There is still time for me to succeed. I will find meaning in these events. I am not a victim. I consciously choose to be in the company of supportive people. I accept life's challenges.

Risk tolerance. Tolerance is inversely correlated to the amount of risk. For prudent people, as risk increases, tolerance decreases. So one essential element of assessing risk tolerance is discerning what's at stake and the probability that one will lose it as opposed to what's to gain and the probability that one will gain it. If there is little at stake, and one is adverse to losing even that small amount, then that person has a low tolerance for risk. If there is a substantial amount at stake, and one can envision losing it and being able to rebound easily, that personal has a high tolerance for risk. "People with survivor personalities like to challenge themselves. They take risks knowing that if they make mistakes they will learn from the experience. They like to put themselves into the unknown to discover how they will handle it. Survivors are self-actualizing. It is the experience of going into the unknown, expecting to find a way to make things work out well, that gives them the survivor orientation in a crisis. The paradox is that self-actualizing people survive better than people whose main concerns are safety and security," says author and professional speaker Al Siebert.

Vision. When one can picture the future as one would like it to be, it is then possible to create a plan for achieving that future. It is sort of like remembering how something is, before it actually happens. Seeing the picture clearly, in detail, makes it possible to also see what steps will lead from the present to the envisioned future. The process is called proactive futuring or visualization.

Willingness to seek advice and assistance. There is so much business information available today, and not nearly enough time to become an expert in every discipline. Therefore, it becomes crucial to form alliances with competent professionals with whom we feel comfortable in self-disclosure, and who champion our vision and our goals. Imbedded in the process of building alliances is the necessity to let go of the need to be right. Robert Lussier reported in the Journal of Strategic Business Management, January 1995, that successful firms made greater use of professional advice and developed more specific business plans.

Summarize The Results

After you have collected all the evaluations, calculate the average value assigned to each attribute. As you calculate these averages, be on the lookout for any response that is uniquely out of line from all the other responses. If the respondent did not provide a concrete example that would explain the substantial deviation, you may be justified in disregarding it. (You may have noticed that in some athletic contests, six or seven judges score a contestant and the lowest score is discarded). A dramatic deviation could happen a few times in the summarizing phase. Use your best judgment in calculating the averages. Remember, you are conducting this survey to acquire information that will help you make a decision that could have a significant impact on your life.

Record these averages on a master copy of the table so that you will have a visual reference. If you find that most of your attributes fall consistently above the sixth level on the scale, you will have some powerful assurance that you possess the qualities that predict success in business ownership.

If you find that in many areas your attributes fall around the middle of the scale, acknowledge the red flag and dedicate yourself to conducting an even deeper evaluation of your desire to own a business and your potential for success. After you have finished reading this book and have a comprehensive understanding of the requirements of business ownership, expand discussions with friends and family about what it means and how it will impact all of you. Consider seeking advice from a professional coach or a career counselor to investigate further your propensity for ownership.

If many or most of your scores fall below four on the scale, you should probably give serious consideration to whether the fulfillment of your business ownership dream is worth the risk you will be assuming (See Chapter Three).

There are excellent assessment tools which provide reliable information upon which to base your decision. Anyone who will be undertaking a significant amount of risk may want to invest in consultation with a career counselor. Check the Yellow Pages for the names of outplacement firms or professional career counselors. The cost of securing an evaluation of your entrepreneurial aptitude is infinitesimally small when compared to the costs of a disastrous sojourn into a venture for which you are ill-suited. A slow spiral into bankruptcy, the loss of friends, or the devastating end of a marriage can irrevocably damage a life.

Complementary Skills and Attributes

Entrepreneurship is the pursuit of opportunity even when there are limited resources available. So let me suggest an option for you to consider if you feel a little shaky about the suitability of your personal resources for business ownership. Is there someone whose skills and attributes complement yours and with whom you could join forces to build a successful business? There are very powerful benefits that result from forming joint ventures: reduced capital investment burden or increased capital available for start up costs, reduced risk exposure, greater opportunities for brainstorming and creative problem solving, and shared responsibility for the work of the business owner are just a few of the benefits. If you decide to build a business with someone else, it is very important that you consult a certified public accountant (CPA) and an attorney to discuss the various legal and tax considerations for the form your business will take — partnership, limited liability partnership (LLP), corporation (S or C) or limited liability company (LLC). You will also want to discuss succession planning with your attorney and consider key man insurance to ensure that the business can continue should something happen to one of you.

After I earned my master's degree, I was thrilled to have an opportunity to work for Michael Gerber, author of The E Myth (number one on my recommended reading list for anyone considering building a business). Michael introduced me to the concept of turnkey operations and the value they create for franchises. A couple of years later, when I was chomping at the bit to have my own business, I began researching franchises. I felt strongly that the kind of business wasn't acutely important to me, because I wanted to do the work of the owner. So after lengthy research and a thorough due diligence, I decided to buy an interior decorating franchise.

Most of the other franchises in my region were operated by talented decorators who loved interior design but cared little for the work of the owner, while I loved developing and implementing marketing and business development strategies. Most of us worked long hours in order to accomplish everything that had to be done, and while we felt satisfied by some aspects of our businesses, we were also frustrated by others. And so one day it just sort of happened: one of the other franchisees, Janet, and I decided to combine our two franchises in order to capitalize on each of our strengths. I would do the administrative, marketing and financial work of the two franchises; after all, I had a background in business management and entrepreneurship. Janet would do the operations work because she is a gifted designer who has gone on to win national recognition for her designs and continues to this day to practice her art.

We sought and received approval from the franchiser and our regional directors, met with our separate accountants to work through our financial reporting requirements, and retained an attorney to draw up a legal agreement between the two of us. Eureka! The result was that we created success for everyone. Janet and I loved the work we were doing, our attitudes were positive, our business benefited from a full-time manager and best of all, our clients benefited by having the best possible interior decorating service.

Hardship teaches that the attitudes and skills of the entrepreneur are the essential ingredients that will make it possible to overcome the most challenging obstacles, and the degree to which we possess positive attitudes and strong skills predicts how well we will travel the road to success.

Table of Attributes

Attribute	Degree to which you possess the attribute									
	1	2	3	4	5	6	7	8	9	10
Ability/willingness to delegate										
Ability to self-manage effectively										
Ability/willingness to negotiate										
Assertiveness (ability to confront issues)										
Commitment										
Conclusiveness										
Creativity										
Desire to learn and grow/curiosity										
Energy/stamina/health										
Exhuberance										
Flexibility										
Focus/clarity										
Genuine regard for people										
Good communicator										
Life Balance										
Openness/self-disclosing										
Optimism										
Organizational ability										
Passion										
Perseverence/persistence										
Personal sense of well being										
Problem solving ability										
Resilience										
Risk tolerance										
Vision										
Willingness to seek advice and assistance										

3

Conduct a Feasibility Study

Now that you have taken a look at your personal values, goals and attributes (the internal factors that greatly influence the success of your venture) it's time to take a look at the external factors that will impact your business. The process you are about to embark upon is called a feasibility study, or due diligence, and it is one of the most interesting, rewarding and stimulating activities an entrepreneur can undertake.

You probably have many ideas swimming in your head about how your business will look and operate, and who it will serve. Now is the time for you to validate your beliefs about the business by finding other companies that provide identical, or nearly identical, products or services. This adventure of discovery will take you outside your present community (would you really want to help a competitor get a foothold in the same community?) and give you an opportunity to learn all the positive and negative aspects of the business you envision.

Ichak Adizes compares the feasibility stage of business development to the courtship before marriage in a November, 1996 article in Inc. magazine. "In the courtship stage of the life cycle, it's normal to have doubts about whether or not your business idea will become a reality. Anyone who's ever passed through this stage before the company actually exists — when the emphasis is on ideas and possibilities — has had doubts. But how do you know which doubts are normal when starting a business? You can find out by doing some serious reality testing, which you can begin by answering these questions: 1) What exactly are we going to do? 2) How is it going to be done? 3) Who is going to do it and why?

"If a business isn't tested during the courtship stage, the founder's commitment remains untried and might not be strong enough to sustain a growing company. At the first sign of trouble, the entrepreneur's commitment could evaporate. The business could have pathological problems that go unnoticed because no hard-nosed questions are asked. The entrepreneur's plans could be based on his or her fantasies of how things should be, not on what is. If that is the case, the idea will remain at the fantasy level and won't grow to an operational level. The courtship will end up being nothing but a passing affair."

Identifying Similar Businesses

Begin by making a trip to your local library to become

acquainted with your reference librarian. This person will be a priceless resource for you as your embark upon your business development path. Ask the librarian to help you determine the SIC code for your intended business by using the Standard Industrial Classification Manual, published by the Office of Budget and Management. All major industries in the United States have been assigned a SIC code. There are numerous business directories in the reference section of the library which you can use to locate other businesses with the same SIC code. Some of them provide such valuable information as number of employees, years in business, and annual revenue. Now narrow your search to communities that are near you. For instance, I live in Portland, Oregon. I would look for similar businesses that are located in Salem, Eugene, Bend or Medford, Oregon or possibly in Seattle, Washington. I wouldn't choose a business in Atlanta or New York for a couple of reasons. First, both cities are located so far from me that the cost of my due diligence would be prohibitive. In addition, the various regions of the country have very different cultures, which means that the markets for those regions could be very different from the market in Portland.

Establishing a Connection

Next, send a letter to each of the identified businesses. Don't be reluctant to send a letter to the owner of every business you locate, because you want to establish contact with one or more who are thriving and willing to allow you to visit. In your letter, explain that you are considering opening a similar business in your community and that you are conducting a due diligence. Explain that you will call within a few days to see if you could take the owner to breakfast or lunch. Be very forthright — tell the owner that you have questions you would like to ask about his/her experience.

One week later call every owner to whom you wrote. If you sent five letters, and the first two owners you contact by phone grant an appointment, do not abandon your follow-up calls for two reasons. First, if you have not already developed the habit of keeping your commitments, now is the time to do it! Second, if you happen to end up with five appointments, your due diligence will be the richer and more accurate for your extensive research. Experience suggests, however, that you will probably end up with one appointment for every five to ten letters sent. I suggest that you attempt to secure at least three appointments.

During your telephone conversations with these owners, you will want to consciously practice your listening skills, and purposely suppress your desire to talk. You are listening for each owner's attitudes toward the business and his or her openness to sharing experiences with you. If both are positive, you will want to establish a connection — a mutual interest that will provide a common ground when you meet in person. If you perceive a negative attitude, listen to see if you can discern why. Is the pessimism an indicator of a pitfall of this type of venture? Or is it indicative of the personality of the owner? Do you remember the two printing franchise owners mentioned in Chapter One? While one was miserable and failing, the other was enthusiastic and her business is thriving. One of the reasons for interviewing three or more owners is to get a clear sense of the what the ownership experience would be like for you; to strip away any distortion of reality.

Make appointments to visit each owner. I personally like to schedule breakfast meetings whenever possible because it facilitates talking with the owner when he or she is fresh and alert, before any fires can crop up to demand his/her attention. You, of course, will be picking up the tab for the meal. While it is seldom important to take the owner to the fanciest restaurant in town, be sure you make reservations at some place where the ambiance is conducive to a serious discussion. Remember, you are asking this owner to give you something of value — information. Don't skimp! Show your respect for his or her time. Ask the owner if you could visit the business establishment after breakfast for a tour. The first-hand information you gather during your visit will open your eyes to challenges and possibilities you probably could not imagine.

Formulating Questions

One means of showing respect for the owner's time is to do your homework before your meeting, so that you will come prepared with thoughtful questions that will give you the information you need, but not ask the owner to divulge highly confidential information.

Doing your homework requires a trip back to the library. First, see if you can locate any articles about the individual business you will visit. Then read every article about the industry you are considering (you may very well have done this research when you first got the entrepreneurial twinkle in your eye). These articles will probably inspire some questions you will want to pose.

In addition, you will find a wonderful publication in the reference department, the Robert Morris Associates' Annual Statement Studies. This annual publication contains composite financial data, including commonly used ratios, on manufacturing, wholesaling, retailing, service, agriculture and contracting lines of business. It presents an opportunity for you to determine what industry averages are for the business you plan to undertake. It also furnishes you with data that will comprise some of the questions you will want to ask the business owners you interview.

I wish I had a dollar for every time I had heard that a business failed because it was undercapitalized. Undercapitalization is one of the symptoms of a failing business — but it is rarely the cause for failure. It is much more likely that the cause was poor anticipation of the financial needs of the business, poor planning for success, or poor management of resources. It is during the due diligence process that you will begin to estimate the capital you will need to start and operate your business until it can consistently produce the level of revenue necessary to be self-sustaining. One of the most efficient and accurate means of estimating your capital needs is to ask those owners who have gone before you. Once you have identified several owners who are willing to share the story of their success (or failure) with you, you will want to ask them the most precise questions possible about the financial aspects of starting and operating their businesses.

It would not be appropriate to list here all the questions you will want to ask the business owners you interview. That kind of cookie cutter approach can't begin to capture the essence of what you will want to learn from your investigation. However, here are a few discovery guideline suggestions:

1. KISS — Keep It Short & Simple. Begin by identifying the major areas of inquiry. Then formulate a few questions that will give you insight into each area. The initial meeting with an owner, possibly the first of several, affords an opportunity to develop esprit de corps and build trust. If you ask too many questions, or probe too deeply, the owner might become uncomfortable. You may choose to develop a

long list of questions, prioritize the queries, and then ask only the first few, most important questions unless you and the owner develop a particularly trusting rapport.

2. Begin by exploring the questions that are least confidential and intrusive, giving the owner time to assess his/her comfort level with you and your inquiry. The inquiry might proceed in this order:

a. Questions about the history of the business: when was the business started? did the owner start or purchase the business? are there associates? has the business always been in the same location, etc.?

b. Who does the owner consult as advisors: CPA, attorney, business and/or marketing consultants, board of advisors or directors, investors?

c. What kind of time commitment does the owner normally make to the business: number of days per week, hours per day, vacations and holidays?

d. Is there a business plan, either formal (the kind used to obtain financing) or strategic (the kind used to guide the owner toward stated goals)? How about a mission statement? What is the owner's vision for the future of the business?

e. Is there a sales and marketing plan, either formal or informal? Has the owner identified a particular market segment? What is unique about this business? How many customers does his business have? What is the maximum number that could be served? What strategies does the owner use to gain customers? Is advertising budgeted? What percentage of revenue is earmarked for marketing? For generating sales? Is networking a specific strategy?

f. What is the customer service policy of the business? How does the business determine the level of customer satisfaction?

g. Finally, begin making inquiries into the financial aspects of the business only after developing a comfortable relationship. If you do not feel that you have developed a trusting relationship with an owner, tread very lightly into the financial arena, keeping your inquiries broad and non-invasive. (One reason it is important to interview numerous owners is that not every interview will result in a camaraderie between parties. You may need to interview four or five owners before you find one who is open to sharing detailed financial information.) It may be easiest to begin with simple questions about start up costs, projections and how well actual financial performance conformed to those projections. Can the owner identify any particular pitfalls to watch for? Is the owner willing to provide you with a copy of the chart of accounts for the business? It may not be appropriate to request copies of financial statements, but the chart of accounts will give you a good idea of the sources of revenue and kinds of expenses this business recognizes. Is the owner willing to share information about gross profit margins? Net profitability percentage?

3. Take written questions with you, carefully and neatly typed, with space after each question to make notations about the answers offered by the owner. Ask the owner for permission to make notes about his/her comments. This is a definite must — failure to do so could hinder building the level of trust necessary to get candid answers to some of your more sensitive questions.

4. Listen, listen, listen. This is not the time to impress the owner with the greatness of your ideas for building your business. Your purpose is to uncover as many details as possible about his/her experience, good or bad, so that you can determine whether this business is a good fit for you. In addition to listening to the words the owner uses, listen for

the emotion that underlies the words. Observe the body language. How does he or she feel about owning the business — enthusiastic, proud, excited, eager, energetic or tired, pessimistic, discouraged?

5. Be self-disclosing when it's your turn to talk. One of the quickest ways to build trust is to be open and forthright. If your demeanor is closed-lipped or secretive, do not expect the person you are interviewing to lay his/her cards on the table for you. Secretiveness on your part will engender suspicion and concern on the part of the person being interviewed.

After you have developed your questions and prepared a plan for conducting the interview, practice with friends. Tape your practice sessions so you can hear how you come across to the other person (if you have the equipment available, videotape the sessions for feedback on your body language). Remember that old 360-degree feedback process — it's time to bring that tool out of your toolkit again.

Here's a clue. If you find that there is too much effort involved in this process and you feel some resentment about the suggestion that you follow it in such detail, take time to reflect again on your desire to go into business for yourself. The tools outlined in this book are the tools used by successful business owners. Do you plan to be successful?

By the time you have completed three interviews, you should have a pretty clear idea of whether there is a good fit between your vision for your business and reality. I do not mean to imply that your business will be a mirror image of any of the companies you have interviewed. However, the work these owners do will be a good predictor of the work you will be doing. You may decide to take your business to new levels of productivity and service, or you may plan to operate a smaller version of the companies you see. But most assuredly, the work will be similar enough that you can get a feel for whether it will bring you satisfaction.

Checking Out Your Marketplace

Now it is time to take a close look at the elements of your marketplace to see if there is a need for the product or service you intend to offer and whether consumers will pay enough money for your product or service for you to be profitable.

Begin by using the Yellow Pages of your phone book, or the assistance of the librarian, to identify all the companies in your market that sell the same product or service. Research the age, number of employees, annual revenue, profitability, target market, etc. of each of these companies. You will need to do substantial pencil and paper figuring to determine how many customers each of those companies probably has (use the data gathered from your earlier interviews). This process is much easier if you plan to serve a geographically small market. Can you imagine what this process is like if you want to launch a new business that serves a worldwide customer base over the internet? (If the second example matches your dream, you will most likely want to seek the services of a consultant whose expertise is internet marketing. Be sure you interview several consultants, ask for references, and conduct a due diligence with those references!)

After you determine how many customers each business probably has, or could have, determine what percentage of the population in your market area is being served. Is the market already saturated or is there room for another supplier in the market? If there aren't enough suppliers to fill the needs of the target population, entry into the market is
relatively uncomplicated.

However, it's tricky to enter a market that already appears heavily saturated. There is usually room for another supplier when it offers something that will distinguish it from what's already available. Will you offer a better product? Do you plan to have a new delivery channel for your product or service? Will you offer "knock your socks off" service?

The November 4, 1996 issue of Forbes magazine was devoted to "The Best Small Companies in America." One of them was Safeskin Corp.: "The defining moment in Richard Jaffe's career came in 1987, when the Centers for Disease Control issued an alert advising doctors, nurses and dentists to protect themselves from their patients' body fluids. As fear of the AIDS virus spread, the demand for disposable latex gloves skyrocketed.

"Today Jaffe's Safeskin Corp. is the number one seller of latex exam gloves in the $500 million U.S. acute care market, with a 25 percent share.

"When he and his partner, an engineer named Neil Braverman, entered the latex glove market in 1988, demand was so heated that there was a severe shortage. But instead of simply copying big manufacturers like Baxter Healthcare, Johnson & Johnson and Ansell, Jaffe was determined to differentiate his gloves. He spoke to health care workers who were wearing gloves for ten hours a day, versus just a few minutes at a time before the AIDS scare hit.

"'I realized that if you put anything against your skin for that long, you are going to get sick, with allergic reactions and dermatitis,' says Jaffe.

"So Jaffe and Braverman built a factory in Malaysia to produce gloves designed to prevent the allergic reactions many doctors were complaining about. Great idea, but by the time they introduced their first hypoallergenic latex gloves in 1989, the previous year's shortage had turned into a flood. 'We had manufactured 200 million gloves, but we had no customers, no distribution and there was a two-year glut on hand,' says Jaffe. 'We dug a pretty deep hole for ourselves.'

"It took three years for Safeskin to climb out of that hole. Jaffe saved himself by opening new distribution channels. He bypassed traditional distributors and hired top salesmen from operations like U.S. Surgical and Johnson & Johnson who had contacts among doctors and other health care workers using gloves. To educate regulators and doctors on the difference between his latex gloves and his competitors' less expensive gloves, Jaffe hired a well-respected doctor.

"Smart work. By going straight to the doctors, Jaffe created a grassroots demand for his high-priced gloves. Jaffee figured correctly that demand from doctors would make hospitals willing to bypass their penny-pinching administrators and pay a premium." It is possible to succeed in a saturated market if you differentiate your business, giving customers a solid reason to leave their current supplier.

In conducting your feasibility study, look to the future as well as the present. Visit your local government planning offices to study planned and/or proposed development for your area. Are there intended or actual zone changes in the works? Will urban growth boundaries be expanded? What road and highway improvements are scheduled? Even if you work out of a home office and think that these things have no effect on you, they may have an effect on your target market.

Finally, contact a representative sampling of prospective customers. If your clients are other businesses, call the person in each company responsible for purchasing. If your clients are individuals, you may need to be creative about conducting your survey. You may choose to contact them by telephone, or by canvassing a neighborhood, knocking on doors.

Years ago I heard about a woman who was considering marketing her services as an appearance consultant to professionals. She took a clipboard full of survey forms to a busy downtown corner and surveyed professional people as they walked down the street. As a result of the information she gathered, she eventually targeted a niche market, banks, and proceeded to build a successful business conducting seminars for customer service representatives.

If your prospective venture is fairly risky (see Chapter Four) you may decide to hire a professional market researcher. Just be sure you test the waters before you jump in. Wilson Harrell warns in his article "Shrink to Fit," printed in the November, 1997 issue of Success magazine, "Now don't go quitting your job, mortgaging your house, or borrowing money from Mama and Papa. Test the market first. Put on your selling shoes and visit a few [potential customers]. Offer them such a deal that they can't say no...If the first prospect says no, go to the next and the next."

A word of caution about feasibility studies. If this product or service you envision is one that may become intensely competitive with existing suppliers, it is quite certain that you will be rebuffed by managers of potential competitors who would view providing you confidential information as creating unfair advantage. No shrewd operator is going to openly give you an edge, particularly if he estimates that you may become a serious contender for business he does not wish to share.

However, there are other sources that can provide you with significant information in the absence of cooperation from wary businesses already established in your prospective field. Chief among these are industry magazines or journals, which report business successes, trends, new ideas, product descriptions, promotions, marketing plans, advertising budgets, company and industry sales and earnings as part of a continuing interpretation and reporting function designed to inform its industry readership of marketing changes, opportunities, and success stories of products.

Such magazines or journals usually are vital information sources from which investigators can form reliable opinions to be used in feasibility planning.

4

Assess the Risk

Growing a successful business will have a price. You must determine if you are willing and able to pay that price, and if the prize at the end is an adequate trade-off for it. "You gain strength, courage and confidence by every experience in which you really stop to look fear in the face. You are able to say to yourself, 'I lived through this horror. I can take the next thing that comes along.' You must do the thing you think you cannot do," said the indomitable Eleanor Roosevelt.

When we take a risk, meet challenges head on, and overcome obstacles, we emerge with greater self-confidence and self-esteem, which in turn empower us to meet additional challenges. When you review your life, what has been your personal history of risk taking. Al Siebert, author of an article entitled "The Survivor Personality," tells us:

"People whose fear of risk and loss prevents them from taking new actions or having new experiences don't survive well. They are easily threatened. They are afraid they may look foolish. They clutch up when loss may occur. They founder when dealing with the unknown.

"Thus, the best way to develop a survivor personality is to be less concerned about safety and security and more oriented toward discovering more of you. Be less concerned about looking foolish and more with having fun.

"All significant learning is based on experiences. Thus, the first step is to do something...the people who made things work out in the Depression were people with nerve. First they used their imaginations to develop creative ideas. Then they had enough nerve to try something new, something that might work out."

Have you been cautious in your approach to life? Or have you been bold, willing to take on new ventures because you understand that if they don't work out, you will have learned something from the experience that you will be able to use in the future?

Let's look at a few of the specific areas in which business owners face uncertainty.

Financial Risk

This is a good place to discuss the amount of financial risk that is involved in owning a business, because it varies widely, depending upon the kind of business, your age, the number of people involved, the location and many other factors. For instance, if you are considering starting a home-based business that does not require you to purchase costly equipment or materials, in which you will be the only employee, and which you can operate in off hours from another job, the financial risk factor is very low. On the other hand, if you want to operate a manufacturing business, which requires the purchase or lease of a sizable facility and costly equipment, the employment of several people, and your full-time commitment to the operation, your risk factor is quite high. The more capital it takes to start and the more revenue it takes to operate, the higher the financial risk factor of any new venture.

Risk is part of owning a business. But as General George Patton said, "Taking calculated risks is quite different from being rash." You are going to examine the risk involved in starting or buying a business in order to take the gamble and rashness out of your decision.

Step 1:   How much money will it take to start your business and how will you provide the financing? Now that you have conducted your feasibility study (Chapter Three), you have a preliminary, fairly reliable understanding of how much money it will take to start your business and to keep it operating for the first few years. I recommend that, until you have completed your strategic planning process, you multiply your anticipated financial needs by a factor of 1.5. Overestimating the capital needs of a start up may give you cause to reconsider, but it won't get you into serious trouble. Underestimating capital needs can be calamitous.

What will be the source of your seed money? If you have enough money saved to fund your start up, what would be the impact upon you personally and upon your family if you should lose those savings?

Some entrepreneurs choose to fund their start up businesses with money they have saved for retirement. If this is your plan, do you have enough working years ahead of you to be able to replace that money before your planned retirement date?

The following advice was written by Meg Whittemore in the November 1997 issue of Success magazine, for people planning to purchase a franchise, but it holds true for anyone who plans to start a new business. "Don't plunge right in. The advice we're about to give may seem obvious, but many franchisees fail to heed it...make sure you can afford to stay in business long enough to start breaking even. To figure out whether you're well prepared, first add up all the costs of staying in business for at least six months. Then, factor in at least six months' worth of living expenses and a contingency fund that you can use if the economy softens or unforeseen disaster hits. If you don't have that kind of cash, it's time to go back to raising money.

"Don't bet the farm. Stay away from retirement funds, set-aside accounts for your health care, college funds, and life-insurance policies.

"Don't run up your credit cards. This is expensive money. Some franchisees use cash advances to get through periods when things are tight, but this is risky, and it's too easy to get into trouble."

I agree in principle with Whittemore's suggestions, but encourage you to use twelve months, rather than six, as your yardstick.

If you are funding your venture with borrowed funds, how will you secure the loan? Banks and other professional lenders will require sufficient collateral to pay off the loan in full — and they almost always require the personal guarantee of borrowers. What would be the result of defaulting on a loan? Are you prepared to accept that result?

Step 2:   How comfortable are you with investing money? Here's the thing about the money that will be used to build your business: it is an investment. It is money that you will use to produce more money. Earning an adequate

return on your investment of at least a few points over inflation is one of the two primary reasons for going into business (the other is answering a consumer need — and who
would want to answer a need with a solution that didn't also
produce an adequate return on investment?). So in assessing
your financial risk tolerance, look at your past investing
behavior. Has it been more important for you to have the
security of a less risky investment (savings account, CD)
than to have a high yielding return (stocks, bonds, etc.)?
Financial planners have questionnaires they routinely
administer to clients to assess their risk tolerance/aversion.
If you have never taken one of these surveys, it would probably be wise for you to ask your financial planner to give
you one now.

Step 3:   Would you consider funding your venture
with equity financing, giving up some share of the ownership
and profits? If you find that you are somewhat risk averse,
this may be an acceptable means of securing the money you
need. There are, of course, trade-offs. The great news is that
if you are able to convince an investor of the value of your
venture and that person prudently conducts his/her own due
diligence, you have twice as much reason to anticipate success. In addition, you will also have formed a bond with
another person who will be as enthusiastic and eager about
the venture as you are — someone you can brainstorm with,
bounce ideas off, and count on to be your cheerleader as you
transform your dream, your commitment, your energy and
your skill into a solid, growing, profitable business.

On the other hand, you will then have to share your profitability with your equity partner. And, depending upon the
amount of financing you require, you may have to give up
considerable control of how you grow your company. If you
choose to utilize equity financing, it is essential that you and

your investor consult an attorney and a CPA to establish the proper legal/tax entity.

After you have worked through these three steps, you should have a good sense of your willingness to assume the financial risk of starting a business, and how well you would deal with a financial setback, should one occur. Al Siebert reminds us, "...survivors don't get angry at the world for not treating them better. They can let go and start over. Thus when an emergency hits they reflexively reach inside themselves to find some way to turn things around."

Jim Cover demonstrated this rebound ability after fire claimed his Montana furniture manufacturing business. Jim's wife, Stacee, had supported the family while he studied engineering at the University of Montana at Bozeman. Jim had been able to cover tuition costs with his popular and sought-after furniture creations. Eventually, the demand for his furniture was so convincing he decided to leave the university and build a manufacturing company. His staff of one grew to twenty, and expansion dictated that the business move from his garage into a two-story factory in Bozeman.

The early morning blaze that brought his business down was ignited by a spark from a faulty furnace. Three hundred thousand gallons of water from the ring of fire trucks around the building could not quench the fire. When the roof collapsed, three truckloads of furniture were destroyed. Jim and Stacee silently huddled together and watched in desperation from the muffler shop across the street.

"This was my entire life," Jim explained, realizing his insurance policy would not cover the costs of rebuilding the factory. It would not even adequately support his family. Jim went home to grieve and make alternative plans. Three or four times a day, however, employees stopped by trying to persuade him to re-open the factory. Long-time, loyal customers pressed checks into his hand saying, "Just fill this order when you can."

Jim could no longer escape making a decision. He decided to go for broke. "Bozeman is a small town and needs my business," he explained. But rebuilding wasn't going to come easy. Jim took the $105,000 from the insurance policy and began paying bills. Unfortunately, he ran out of cash before he ran out of bills. "We couldn't even pay our current debt."

There were $100,000 worth of orders, though, that "were good as gold, but I had no way to fill them." Local businessmen helped the Covers identify and apply for a Community Development Block Grant. Normally the funds from this grant were allocated to expand or start a business, but an exception was made and the grant was approved for $100,000.

Jim began immediately, hiring most of the craftsmen to convert an old Bozeman building into a modern, insulated plant. By early spring, four months after the fire, the first pieces of furniture came off the line. Current sales are around three million dollars, twice the pre-fire revenue. Although Jim Cover's fear of fire will never completely disappear, neither will his appreciation for the people in his community. "I found my determination in their hope."

Putting Your Good Name on the Line

There are other risks associated with failure — risks that are less tangible and concrete than money. One is your name. If your personal name is associated with your business, and that business fails, what happens to the public perception of your name, and you? If you put your name on your business and it turned out that ownership was not a satisfying experience, how willing would you be to close that business? Could you separate your own sense of well-being and self-esteem from the business entity?

I know an owner who has been in business for seven years but has never been profitable. In examining her options for the future of her business, she admits that the thought of closing it is distressing. Her name is on her business. Some of her self-concept is tied up in being a business owner. She is proud to say she owns a business, and she enjoys associating with other business owners. She has become very involved with several organizations whose members recognize her as an owner, and she has always "walked and talked" like a successful entrepreneur. Her associates and comrades have no idea that her business trembles on the brink of closure. The prospect of closing the business and losing her status prevents her from walking away. Instead, she has decided that she prefers to work at developing the skills of an owner, and to build a successful venture. "Nothing splendid has ever been achieved except by those who dared believe that something inside them was superior to circumstance," observed Bruce Barton.

It is possible to eliminate or at least reduce risk by not associating your name with the name of your business. But there are trade-offs for this strategy. If you are highly regarded in the community for the work you have done with another company, you may want to capitalize on that reputation by using your name to draw customers.

Risking Your Reputation

There is also potential for risk to your reputation — separate from your name. If you operate a business in the same industry that you have worked in in the past, and that you would probably return to if you closed your business, what impact would a business failure have on your reputation in that industry and on your ability to find future employment with other companies in that industry? In many communities, suppliers and competitors know most of the "players" in a given industry. If your business should not provide you with the level of satisfaction you hope for and need, would those suppliers or competitors be willing to offer you positions in their companies?

A Blow to Self-Esteem

Finally, with few exceptions, a business failure gravely undermines one's self-esteem. True entrepreneurs bounce back with yet another venture. Remember the comment attributed to Thomas Edison, when he was asked why he didn't give up trying to invent an incandescent light bulb after a thousand failed attempts. He is reported to have said, "Young man, you don't understand the way the world works. I have just successfully identified hundreds of ways you cannot make an incandescent bulb."

It is very natural, however, to feel a sense of inadequacy when a business fails. Hendrix Niemann found the words to capture the feelings in his article, "The End of the Story," which appeared in Inc. magazine, October 1997. "As my friends came to help I was embarrassed to have them see the condition of my company. Like the former owner, I no longer had noticed the dirt, the grease, the grime, the disorganization. I had allowed the men's offices, their desks, their vans to become no better than the inside of garbage cans. I had let the shop remain in a state of chaos since we had moved there, in April 1991. Even though friends were coming out of the woodwork to help us, with no thought to their own schedules or priorities, I got more and more depressed. The enormity of my mismanagement and the scope of my incompetence overwhelmed and all but defeated me."

Although Niemann was forced to close his business, he did not retract or beat himself up. Instead, he counted his blessings — his faith, supporting family and compassionate friends. He "pulled himself up by the bootstraps" as the saying goes, and moved forward with new challenges. The fact that he was able to recount his discouraging venture is a great tribute to his strong sense of self.

Al Siebert says, "The secret ingredient, if it can be called that, is that surviving difficulty comes more from an orientation, an attitude, an expectation than from any specific element. It is the intention to survive and to do so in good shape that brings it all together.

"This is an emotional commitment of the total self. Once made, the how of survival is to be discovered. When problems or setbacks occur they don't waste time moaning. They don't waste time dwelling on the past or on what they've lost. Their energies are directed to getting things to turn out well."

The statement above is certainly true of Wallace Dodge, who years ago sifted through the ashes of his small woodworking plant which had burned to the ground the night before. There was a certain irony, he thought, to the timing of the fire. It happened on the Fourth of July, which was his birthday.

He had no insurance. The little woodworking plant he owned had been small, but fairly prosperous. Now it was a shell of scorched timbers, blackened uprights and partially burned debris. Somewhere he would find the money to start over. His cash reserves were limited and he knew that a tough and bitter struggle lay ahead of him. But there was no doubt in his mind that he would rebuild the plant. Of that he was positive. Right now his job was to sift through what remained to see if there was anything left that he could use in rebuilding.

As he poked through the cinders, charcoal dust settled in his hair and his face and his hands soon turned sooty and black. Before long he came upon a partially burned wooden shaft pulley, carried it off and placed it carefully on the scorched grass. Soon, he found another partially burned pulley of the same size. It joined the first.

One of the workmen who had come to discover whether his job had gone up in smoke snickered to a companion, "What does Wallace want to save them pieces of pulley for? He oughta know that part of a pulley ain't no use."

Wallace Dodge, squatting wearily before his small heap of salvaged materials, was thinking about the same thing.

It was the tradition in woodworking and machinery plants worldwide that wooden shaft pulleys were always made in one piece. They resembled a coin with a hole drilled in the center. They were placed on the main shaft that was driven by the power plant. When it was necessary to change one pulley, the main shaft had to be stopped and all the pulleys removed to reach the defective one. In a large and busy factory, it was a major project, one that consumed time. In addition, while the job was being done, production of each individual machine driven by the main shaft came to a standstill.

Time and time again, on that sultry Fourth of July, Dodge turned the matter of the pulleys over in his mind. Sharpened by adversity, driven by desperation, Dodge eventually hit upon an idea that excited him. Why not, he asked himself, saw away the burned area on each of the pulleys until a perfect half remained, and then place two halves together on the drive shaft and fasten them there? He was a practical man and he knew that he was thinking of something that could be done — but something that had never been done before.

The rest of what happened to Dodge and his idea is history. He proved his theory when the little plant was rebuilt. The salvaged halves of the wood pulleys fitted neatly together and were readily secured to the shaft. He had discovered something that would revolutionize the mechanical transmission of power from a central prime mover to individual machines. It was a scheme that would save work stoppages and endless lost man-hours in busy plants engaged on production schedules of an urgent nature.

Working in a fever night and day, Dodge, inspired and full of confidence, immediately set to work to prove his premise. He made wooden pulleys needed for his shafting — in one piece, according to tradition. Then, to the amazement of the workers and his foreman, he sawed each of them in half. The halves were then fastened to the shaft in the same manner as the burned halves had been installed. The job was done quickly, and the main shaft did not have to be removed from the hangers.

The plan was simple and effective. Wallace H. Dodge obtained a patent and became the world's largest builder of power transmission machinery, a successful and most profitable venture and one which placed the little city of Mishawaka, Indiana, on the industrial map.

Minimize the Risk

Sometimes business owners are served a plate of lemons. The dedicated find a way to minimize their risk by shifting gears and making the famous lemonade. Lois Crandell was entertaining a few of her clients on board her business partner's 60-foot yacht in San Diego Bay. Their consulting company, More Than Money Ventures (MTMV), helped start up companies with business planning and management. They were paid with equity in the businesses they helped, and had earned equity valued at half a million dollars by helping to launch ten new businesses in less than two years. It looked like smooth sailing ahead.

But one night would change all of that. The boat suddenly ran aground, throwing Lois high into the air. She landed on the boat's metal railing and slumped onto the teak deck. Her limp and bloodied body was lowered off the wrecked yacht and rushed to the hospital with serious internal bleeding and multiple hematomas. Her liver was split in two. Doctors worked for hours to save her. Lois peered through the fog of anesthesia and heard a doctor say, "If you want to recover, work is out of the question for the next three years." That's when she knew her life as it had been was over. "I'm going to be poor again," she thought.

The oldest of nine children raised in a small farm town in Wisconsin, Crandell grew up poor. "My parents didn't have the 25 cents necessary to send me to high school basketball games, much less to fund a college education." However, her first-born drive and determination got Lois jobs at high-tech companies in the Minneapolis area. Those same traits pulled her through the ordeal of sudden single parenthood when her husband left her in 1965. She had two children and no means of support. Undaunted, she earned a certificate in electronics by attending night school, worked as a technical writer, and then moved into sales and marketing. She founded her first business, a medical advertising firm, in 1972. She grew it into a three million dollar company and then passed it on to her sister.

In 1988, she was ready to start her dream company, MTMV. She used the managerial and marketing savvy she'd developed throughout her career. If she chose and developed clients carefully, she would build wealth in equity. Her plan had worked. She owned half of MTMV and a portion of three other companies. Not only the yacht, but her dreams were dashed that night in the bay.

Even though Lois's body was broken and in pain, her spirit was indomitable. She made a critical decision, one which brought her a sense of peace. "I decided to put myself in God's hands. There was no more shock or panic. I found that I had lost all fear, even of death."

Still bedridden, she began to study the latest biotechnology journals. In her first year of convalescence, she did part-time consulting between physical therapy appointments. "I worked for mom-and-pop businesses a few hours a week for peanuts, just for money to live on." She was forced to sell her four-bedroom house and virtually all of her possessions. Still she remained buoyant. "I asked myself: 'Is this the worst thing that ever happened to you?' And the answer was no. I overcame the accident, so I can overcome anything."

Lois contacted a leading edge biotechnology company in San Diego. Günter Hoffmann, head of BTX, had lost his wife and co-founder who was responsible for the business side of the enterprise. He hired Crandell for her expertise in entrepreneurial start ups and in medical marketing. She became general manager, president, and finally Chief Executive Officer (CEO). In her first year with BTX, the company's sales increased by thirty-eight percent. The second year they increased by fifty-nine percent. Her equity in company's sales increased by thirty-eight percent. The second year they increased by fifty-nine percent. Her equity in BTX now approaches $1 million. Lois isn't poor anymore. It was Booker T. Washington who said these words that apply to Lois's tough attitude of survival: "Success is to be measured not so much by the position that one has reached in life as by the obstacles which one has overcome while trying to succeed."

There are several ways to minimize risk. One is to share the risk with someone else. As mentioned in Chapter Two, there are numerous advantages to forming joint ventures. Another way to minimize risk is to plan for the success of your venture and to become such a highly skilled owner that your business will provide you with a magnificent level of satisfaction and an appropriate return on your investment.

It was the remarkable risk taker Theodore Roosevelt who captured the essential idea of the entrepreneur: "Far better it is to dare mighty things, to win glorious triumphs even though checkered by failure, than to rank with those poor spirits who neither enjoy nor suffer much because they live in the gray twilight that knows neither victory nor defeat."

5

Formalize Your Vision and Mission

When you first envisioned self-employment, you may
have had only a vague concept of what it would mean.
During the time you conducted your due diligence, visiting
similar businesses and talking with their owners, your head
may have been reeling as thoughts of what your business
would look like began to gel. Perhaps you may have heard
ideas that you hadn't thought of before, but that made sense
to incorporate into your vision. Or you may have even seen
practices that conflict with the image you hold of your successful business. Before you move on in the development of
your business venture, it is crucial that you clarify your
vision.

Fifteen-year-old John Goddard could envision so pre-

cisely what he wanted to accomplish in his lifetime that he wrote a list of the things he was going to do in order to live a completely fulfilling life. His list contained 127 achievements, including these:
- explore the Nile
- circumnavigate the globe
- climb Mt. Everest
- read the entire Encyclopedia Britannica
- write a book
- study primitive tribes in the Sudan
- run a five-minute mile
- read the Bible from cover to cover

Ordinarily we would be inclined to dismiss this list as a teenager's idealistic daydream, except...now middle aged, John Goddard has accomplished almost all of his original goals, plus many more. He is a renowned explorer and author who is actively engaged in turning his childhood vision into reality. Eagerly anticipating the 21st century, he intends to travel to the moon. Can you imagine the joy he must have felt when it was announced that 77-year-old John Glenn would return to space? Who knows, with John Glenn paving the way — John Goddard may yet turn another visualized goal into reality.

Now it is time to clarify your vision of your endeavor, and commit your concept to writing. It isn't enough to have a vague idea of what you want your business to look like, how you want it to perform, how it will treat employees and customers. Peter Senge assures us in The Fifth Discipline, "When there is a genuine vision people excel and learn, not because they are told to, but because they want to."

Have you ever watched a movie that was slightly out of focus, one where you could make out the picture, but you felt anxious and frustrated by the fuzziness, so much so that you found yourself far more involved in your concern about the quality of the picture than in the content of the message? Once the lens was adjusted and the picture became sharp, it was possible to see clearly the image on the screen. You may have felt yourself relax as you lost yourself in the story taking place in the movie, and you no longer needed to expend your concentration and energy fretting over the mechanics of the presentation. If your vision for your business venture is fuzzy, your message to your public will be unpredictable and inconsistent.

Formalizing your vision rarely happens quickly. The process requires brainstorming, drafting and refining, sharing with associates and/or advisors, and finally producing a succinct, clearly worded picture of exactly what your business will look like the day you open the doors and how you expect it to look five years from now.

To ensure that your vision is crystal clear, it needs to be articulated and written. Then it must be understood, committed to, and woven into the fabric of every person who works within your business. If potential associates or employees do not share your vision, no problem — they are welcome to work for some other business. It's that simple. When there is no commitment to the vision, myriad problems emerge, from unsatisfactory performance to sabotage. Remember what Senge said, "When there is a genuine vision people excel and learn, not because they are told to, but because they want to."

When your vision of the business is in complete harmony with your values and when you are fully committed to making that vision come true, you will find that you can accomplish all that you dream and more, just like John Goddard.

We all know that research shows unequivocally that people who write their goals and their vision for the future achieve them. Why?

First, the process of writing requires us to get very clear about what we want. Robert Fritz tells us, "The way to activate the seeds of your creation is by making choices about the results you want to create. When you make a choice, you mobilize vast human energies and resources which otherwise go untapped. All too often people fail to focus their choices upon results and therefore their choices are ineffective."

Second, the very act of writing our goals seals our commitment to them. So let me ask you this: how many of you are fifty percent committed to writing your goals for your business? Eighty percent committed? One hundred percent committed? Remember that commitment, like pregnancy, knows two percentages — 100 and zero.

Third, writing our goals frees our minds for creative thinking. The mind works very hard to hang onto our ideas until it is released from that responsibility. Once you have entrusted information to writing, you give your mind permission to let go. Do you ever find yourself unable to sleep at night because your mind is processing? How do you get back to sleep? If you choose to write your thoughts, your subconscious mind will know it has been given permission to go back to sleep.

When I was in graduate school, I had the great fortune to take classes from Bill Kutz, who is truly gifted at helping clients clarify their visions and their missions. Bill insisted that once his clients had clarified their visions, all of their employees must understand and 'own' those visions. One of my favorite stories told by Bill reflects how powerful a clear vision can be. He was working with a large hotel to improve its image and its revenue. Bill would randomly stop employees he encountered and ask them to recite their mission, which was something like "service that brings customers back." If they couldn't tell him, he immediately went to see the CEO for a chat — an admonishing "trip to the woodshed" that encouraged the CEO to remind all employees of their shared vision. It was not long before everyone working at the hotel understood clearly that their mission was to provide the kind of service that would bring customers back.

One day a custodian was on a ladder replacing a light bulb in the corridor outside some of the guest rooms. He observed a guest emerge from his room with an empty ice bucket and go to the ice machine, only to find that the machine was not working. There was no ice. The disappointed guest returned to his room. The custodian could have chosen to do nothing, to report the broken ice machine or to fix it, and I suspect he did do one of the latter after he had acted in complete compliance with the company mission. First, he went to a supply closet, got another ice bucket, went to a different ice machine, and returned to deliver the full bucket of ice to the grateful and somewhat surprised guest. Wow! Service that brings customers back! Needless to say, this hotel realized substantial growth under Bill's guidance.

The behavior of the custodian was not a surprise to Bill Kutz, nor would it be to anyone who understands the power of a clearly communicated vision. If you grasp this principle, you will easily recognize the importance of formulating a mission statement that can be easily memorized and recited by everyone associated with your venture. You will understand that this empowers you and everyone involved to make the decisions and take the actions that will progress you toward your goals.

Here are the three writing assignments you should complete and file in the binder you are creating for the development of your business:

1. Create a Statement of Values for Your Business

Review the personal values you filed in your workbook. These will provide the foundation for the vision of your endeavors. If the vision for your venture is in complete harmony with your values, you will find that you can never compromise how you will treat customers, suppliers, employees or anyone else in the general public. Many businesses have created a statement of excellence that clearly identifies those values held in common by everyone associated with the business. These statements of excellence frequently affirm how the company will treat customers, employees, competitors and suppliers. They may also address the company's beliefs about quality of product or service, innovation, conservation, commitment to the community, and so forth. Write your statement of values and file it behind the tab "Values/Vision/Mission."

2. Articulate Your Vision for Your Business in the Future

After establishing the foundation of values for your venture, add to that a description of how you envision your venture will look in the future. Who will be involved? What will your role be? How quickly will the venture grow, if growth is a goal? What will be the final disposition of your venture? (It frequently comes as a surprise to people who are just beginning to envision a new venture when they are asked to think about how they will terminate their relationship with their business. But this is the time to be thinking of what the final outcome might be. Do you want to grow a business that you could pass to your children or sell to someone else? Would you like to sell shares of the business to the public?)

Condense your vision into a document no more than one page in length. File this document in your binder behind the tab "Values/Vision/Mission."

3. Write Your Mission Statement

Next encapsulate your vision in one brief statement that can be easily displayed, memorized, committed to, and acted upon. Bill Kutz expressed his strong belief that a mission statement should contain no more than six words. I think the mechanics of the number of words is less significant than the ability of the statement to capture the essence of why you are in business, and to be easily recognized and memorized. I can remember a wonderful illustration that I heard in one of my graduate school classes.

The proprietor of a business that packaged fine art works for shipment around the world was struggling to create a mission statement. He kicked one idea after another around with his consultant, but none seemed to capture the essence of his business. Finally, the consultant asked him why his customers came to him — why they didn't just go to a mail center to have their art works packaged and shipped. Because, he indicated, he had such sophisticated packaging materials and methods that he could guarantee that the art works would arrive at their destination in the same condition they were in before the transfer. His customers enjoyed the peace of mind that came from knowing that their goods would arrive safe and undamaged. "So," the consultant inferred, "what you provide for your customers isn't a packaging and wrapping service, it's a peace of mind service." Bingo. Providing peace of mind became not only his mission, it also became the name of the business, "Peace of Mind Packaging."

I have been blessed with many great opportunities in my life. One of them was working with Jo Rymer-Culver, the creative visionary who is CEO/President of Pro Tem Professional Staffing Services in Portland, Oregon. Jo absolutely honors her values by living them fully, in her personal and professional life. When I started working at Pro Tem, the company had a lengthy mission statement — it was actually a vision statement. I encouraged Jo to consider the power of a succinct mission statement that could be easily memorized and could become the conviction of every employee. She readily embraced the concept. At a weekly staff meeting Jo asked all the staff members to give thought to what the mission should be, and come prepared to discuss their ideas at the next staff meeting.

I can remember that subsequent meeting as clearly as if it occurred yesterday. We all brought several suggestions, some we liked better than others. And after we had all spoken, Jo said she had envisioned a statement over the weekend and wanted to contribute it for consideration. What she suggested was so simple, so concise, so compelling that we all immediately recognized it for its brilliance. Our mission from that day forward was "Create Success."

It was compelling because it perfectly captured exactly what Pro Tem is about. Pro Tem creates success for its clients by filling their need for qualified temporary employees and creates success for its employees by providing them with placement opportunities that match their skills. But the match between the mission statement and reality was intensified by Jo's absolute commitment to creating success.

As a single parent, Jo was intimately acquainted with the difficulties that many of her employees faced trying to work and also handle child care needs. She was so committed to creating success for those working parents, that she created the first child care subsidy offered by any temporary service in the United States. She has been recognized by the Wall Street Journal, among other publications, for this groundbreaking employee benefit.

"Create Success" was easy to memorize and easy to commit to. It also was easy to recall every time we made a decision about which employee would be a perfect match for a job order, a match that would create success for the client and for the employee. It was also a breeze to post wall signs in our offices. Jo went a step further — she created T-shirts which she gave to clients in appreciation for their loyal business, for being partners in creating success for our employees. I still proudly wear my T-shirt (even though I haven't worked for Pro Tem for several years), and I still get lots of positive comments about the powerful mission statement.

You want to formulate a powerful mission statement that captures the essence of your business, one that will tell your customers, your suppliers, your employees, your competition and your community what you stand for and what you are all about! Remember KISS — Keep It Short and Simple. While there is no hard and fast rule about the number of words that comprises an effective mission statement, recognize that wordier statements can sometimes miss the bull's-eye, and are frequently difficult to memorize.

Once you are comfortable that you have an effective mission statement, print it in bold lettering on a sheet of 8 1/2 x 11 paper. You may want to reproduce this paper several times. One copy of the mission statement should be inserted in your binder immediately inside the front cover, another behind the tab "Values/Vision/Mission." If you happen to have a binder with a clear plastic shield over the front, slip your mission statement inside the front sleeve, and the sleeve down the spine if possible. The other copies should be displayed prominently on the walls of your office or business, where everyone who works for you or is a customer or supplier of your business will see it and know instantly what your business stands for. Memorize the statement, and be sure that any associates or employees memorize it and commit to it.

Here are a few more ideas for keeping your mission statement in front of your eyes and the eyes of employees, suppliers and customers all the time:

- Have your mission statement ironed on T-shirts, sweat shirts, baseball caps or headbands for you and employees to wear.
- Have your printer produce one-fourth page scratch tablets with your name and your mission statement. Give them away to customers and prospects. The printer can use sixteen pound paper so that the scratch pads are economical. Every time your customers or prospects write a note, they will see your company name and what you stand for. And who knows who they will hand that note to — now you have increased your exposure without lifting a finger or a phone!
- Add your mission statement in small type (something like eight point, italicized) to your letterhead the next time you order it. Make sure it is also on your envelope and your business cards. If you have a postage meter, add your mission statement to the imprint.
- Add your mission statement to your company name on your door. Place a mission statement placard on the front desk. Write your mission statement on labels and affix them to every phone in the office. Enter your mission statement on the screen saver for your computer(s). Are you beginning to understand why a short and simple mis-

sion statement is the most effective?

Do not change your mission statement unless absolutely necessary. As Orvel Ray Wilson, the guerrilla marketing guru, says of marketing slogans, do not change them even when you get sick to death of them. Because about the time you are getting sick to death of them, your customers are just beginning to identify your business with the slogan. The same thing is true of your mission statement. You may think it is getting old and worn, but that's because you see it hundreds of times every day. Your customers, suppliers and the general public see it infrequently and they will be just beginning to "get" what you're all about!

These are just a few suggestions. You and your associates and employees will probably generate numerous ways to get that statement in front of everyone. The important thing is to never forget what imparts significance to the work that you do.

Susan Taylor, editor-in-chief of *Essence Magazine*, gives us this sensitive and insightful commentary:

"The people we most admire, the great achievers, the geniuses, are passionate about their purpose and believe that life offers unlimited possibilities. These rare individuals don't limit their talent or ingenuity. They use their inventiveness, an attribute that remains virtually dormant in most people but is available to each of us equally.

"As the lives of great achievers show, we can dream and build a world. Or, as is more often the case, we can live without a vision or a belief in our ability and the infinite possibilities of life. Then we never realize our potential."

Part Two

How to Build a Successful, Enduring Business

6

Write Your Plan for Success

You've heard the call, tested the waters and decided to embark upon the journey of business ownership. A wonderful opportunity lies before you, an opportunity to build a business with your stamp on it. A business that will be the embodiment of the things you value and that give you fulfillment. A business that looks exactly as you visualize it.

The challenge is to develop your business in a manner that will yield the highest probability of success and provide the highest quality journey. Perhaps you have an existing business, but want to improve its performance. In either case, the first step toward business success is writing a strategic business plan, because creating and using a strategic plan will have two highly desirable outcomes:

- the increased probability that your business will succeed in achieving its goals, and
- the improved quality of the experience of ownership.

There is overwhelming research in many areas indicating that those who plan, and commit their plans to writing, have a much higher rate of success than those who do not plan. There are numerous examples of how this research is being used to help people achieve success in such areas as athletics, weight management, and sales, to name just a few. Doesn't it make sense to write your plans for developing your business if that accomplishment will increase the likelihood that your business will thrive? As Patricia Schiff Estess reminded us in an article entitled "Survival Training" that appeared in Entrepreneur magazine, "It's not enough to come up with ideas in your strategic planning sessions and then just hope they'll be put in place. The plan needs to be organized in writing."

Smart entrepreneurs plan, not because books and advisors tell them to, but because they realize that planning increases their chances for success. There may be some businesses that succeed even though they have no plan — but they are the exception. One has to wonder where those businesses might be if they had augmented their great business ideas with a written plan.

When you think of a business plan, it may help to envision the battery in your car. Your car is a complex system comprised of many smaller subsystems. The battery is the initial energy source that enables your car to utilize all the other subsystems. Your business is also a complex system composed of many smaller systems. Your strategic business plan is the source of energy that you will plug into every day to get your business up and running. Like your car battery, your business plan is small but very powerful.

There are a few very sophisticated tools you will need to have handy as you begin the process of writing your plan for success — pencil, paper, your three-ring binder with section dividers, and a calculator! Pretty sophisticated, wouldn't you say? If you happen to have a computer equipped with word processing and spreadsheet software, and you feel comfortable using them, your planning process may proceed more quickly than if you write your plan by hand. But the point is, you don't need to have any fancy tools. The key words in "strategic plan" are strategic and plan, and the most important activities in the strategic planning process are researching, assessing, generating ideas, and evaluating the impact of implementing those ideas.

Kinds of Business Plans

Many of the business owners I work with seem a little intimidated by the thought of writing a business plan. Somehow the very name "business plan" conjures up images of a formal document, professionally prepared and filled with information that can only be deciphered by bankers and lawyers. I want to dispel that myth, and maybe this illustration will help.

When I was growing up my mother had a sterling silver coffee service, which was proudly displayed on the buffet in our dining room. I can only remember seeing it used once or twice, but it had a very definite function. It was a symbol of what my parents had attained, and it set a tone of formality.

In the kitchen, we had a stainless steel percolator, which made coffee for breakfast and dinner, and any other time during the day. It was not glamorous, but it was very useful.

There are two kinds of business plans:

• The formal business plan, used to secure financing, is explicit, follows a prescribed format, and has as its p u r - pose demonstrating to potential lenders why they should feel confident about loaning money to an enterprise. If you have been in business for more than a year, your business is financially sound and not heavily leveraged, and you desire to borrow money for expansion, you may need to prepare this kind of business plan.

• The strategic (also called working or operating) business plan is the owner's workhorse. It doesn't need to be fancy or glamorous. It is the result of thorough research; kicking ideas around; brainstorming about different approaches; setting achievable, measurable goals; formulating strategies to achieve those goals; and developing sound financial projections. The form the plan takes isn't important. The learning and work that go into its preparation — researching, considering options, innovating — are what matter because it is through that work that the owner becomes intimately acquainted with every aspect of the business. Someone once said, "The plan is nothing. Planning is everything." It is important to write the plan because we know from research that the act of writing produces within us a high level of commitment, and creates a force that moves us toward accomplishing what we aim for.

Much of the information you will need to include in the formal business plan will be available from your working, strategic plan. I suggest that you create the strategic business plan first, then take it to potential lenders and ask if it will suffice, or if they need a more formal document. Their responses may depend upon a couple of factors: the amount of money you want to borrow, and the institutions you approach for the loan.

In a recent conversation with the lending officer of a

small, local bank, I was told that he would far rather see an informal, carefully researched and considered working plan prepared and presented to him by an owner who was thoroughly familiar with all aspects of the business, than to be presented with a stiff, formal plan from an owner who had outsourced its preparation. Another banker offered this story about an applicant who had brought him a business plan that had been prepared by a third party. In reviewing the numbers, the banker pointed out that while the financial projections were very optimistic, they did not contain a provision for repaying the bank loan. The applicant said there was no problem. He would just give the plan back to the fellow who had prepared it and have him plug in the loan repayment. Needless to say, the banker rejected the application.

There are a number of software packages available for business plan preparation. They may be helpful in providing a structure for your formal plan, but many lenders have expressed concern over the cookie-cutter results. Every plan looks just like every other, and lenders are suspicious that the owner may have only a superficial knowledge of the proposed business.

Your written strategic plan should be a working document detailing how you plan to succeed with your business — your business bible — a plan of action you will adhere to in order to achieve success. "All businesses need a written plan, even if they're not just getting started or trying to raise capital, because management needs a written document against which to judge progress." This was the observation of Scott Clark, in an article "Plucking the Right Tree from the Business Plan Forest," appearing in The Business Journal.

The form your strategic plan will take depends upon the

kind of business, the number of people involved, the location and other factors. For instance, if you plan to operate a business that does not require you to invest heavily in facilities, equipment, personnel, inventory or supplies, your plan may be relatively simple. However, if your proposed business does require heavy investment in any of these, a much more comprehensive plan will be needed to provide structure for the operations and direction for the growth of the business. As a general rule, the more capital it takes to start and the more revenue it takes to operate, the higher the risk factor of any new venture, and the more imperative it is that all aspects of development be extensively addressed in the planning phase.

A strategic plan provides:
• a reality check
• a timetable for business development
• a vehicle for tracking the progress of your business
• a blueprint which can be adjusted
• a starting point for future planning.

The Strategic Planning Process

The process of strategic planning begins with a course of thinking about, researching and evaluating five key questions:
• Where are we right now?
• Where do we want to go?
• How will we get there?
• How much will it cost to get where we want to go?
• Who will do the work to get us there?

In Chapter One you set up a three ring binder with dividers between the sections. You will probably remember that tabs three through seven were labeled with these questions. In Chapter Seven I have provided forms (which you may duplicate and write on) to aid you in completing your analysis. As you work through writing the answers to these questions, file them behind the appropriate tabs.

Throughout the remainder of this chapter you will find many suggested topics to consider as you ponder your responses to these five basic questions. Those topics are not intended to be all inclusive. Instead they are submitted to help you generate your own queries. There is no one set of topics that will fit every business. Your business is unique and you will want to delve into the issues that are pertinent to it. This was the conclusion of Joshua Hyatt in an article, "The Zero-Defect CEO," in Inc. magazine: "'Every year there's a new book that everybody says has the answers,' grumbles Adolph J. Ferro, the CEO of Epitope Inc., a Beaverton, Oregon company that makes a saliva-based test for detecting HIV antibodies. 'I've read them, and I just don't think there's one that applies to my company. I think every company has to write its own book.'"

Bring discipline to your analysis. Look hard at the assumptions that underlie your decisions. Take care in setting your priorities. Recognize that distortions may be caused by your own biases.As a result of your thoroughness, attention to detail, ability to separate emotion from fact, and capacity to visualize the desired outcome, you will distinguish yourself as a business owner who plans to succeed, and you will increase the probability that you will achieve your goal.

Where Are We Right Now?

Here is an opportunity to paint a picture of what the business has going for it right now. If you haven't yet initiated your business, your resources may be limited. But identifying those resources now will aid you in determining your strategies. Ascertain the people involved in the business, provide a situational analysis of your operations and conditions, indicate the source of capital, analyze your strengths and weaknesses, and identify the opportunities and threats to your venture. Before moving toward a desired destination, it is vital to know where you are now.

The People

Who are the owners of the business? What personal attributes and skills do they bring to this venture? What are their personal values and goals? This section should be fairly easy to compile because of the investigative work you did in Chapters One and Two. (You should have already filed the evaluation forms and your list of values and goals behind the first tab of your binder.) This is also the place to evaluate the experience that the owners bring to this venture. How can you capitalize on that experience? Highlight your knowledge and past successes, along with those of your associates. Be open to understanding your own limitations.

Some business ventures will have employees. Identify the positions those employees will hold and indicate what skills they need to possess. Is special technical expertise essential? If you already have employees, what experience do they bring to your venture and how can you capitalize on their background?

Prepare an organization chart for your business. If you have read The E Myth, you may recall that Michael Gerber says even if you are the only person involved in your business, you need to have an organization chart — and your name goes in every box! I couldn't agree more! In Chapter

Nine you will learn about creating descriptions and procedures for each position in your business. For now, create the organization chart with at least these four positions:

Owner (or President/CEO)
Vice President - Sales & Marketing
Vice President - Operations
Vice President - Finance

Facilities and Equipment

Where will your business reside? Do you own or lease the facility? If you lease, what are the terms of the agreement? Do you need specialized equipment? If so, will you own or lease it? What are the terms of any lease agreements? What are the specific capabilities of your facility and your equipment? Commit this information to writing so that you will be able to assess how your facilities and equipment can be utilized to achieve your goals when you get to the strategizing phase. For instance, if your business owns a computer with word-processing, spreadsheet and accounting software, when you begin formulating strategies you will want this information. Can you produce bulk mailings with your system? Will you be able to track cash flow on a daily basis?

Be sure to carefully inventory all of your equipment and identify the capabilities of that equipment. You may want to delegate this responsibility to employees who are most familiar with the equipment. While you are assembling this information, annotate your list with the locations of the operation manuals of each piece of equipment. Some manuals may be located within the equipment (for instance, copiers often have a self-contained compartment for the manual). If manuals do not need to be kept with the equipment, consider creating a file or bookshelf where all manuals can be kept together — down the line this may eliminate the frustration and fear that can accompany a frantic search when a piece of equipment malfunctions. Be sure to create a file for storing warranties and service contracts.

Operations

What is the actual work of your business? What is the product or service you offer? Explain product design and development. Show how your product or service is produced and explain how it will evolve in the future. What problem is solved by using your product or service? What distinguishes your product or service from the others that are available? As David Clark, Vice President of Merchandising for the Toy Division of Target Stores, was quoted in Forbes magazine, "The real opportunity for a small company is to have something different. If it's just a 'me, too,' I'm not into it. It's the several smaller guys I choose that are going to separate us from Wal-Mart or Kmart. I'm looking for small outfits that have something unique and different." Remember, too, the words of Booker T. Washington, "Excellence is to do a common thing in an uncommon way."

How does work proceed from order intake to delivery to the customer? Who does the work each step of the way? What is the period of time from order intake to delivery? These questions apply to your business whether you manufacture, distribute, transport, repair, sell, or otherwise handle products, or provide an intangible service. In the greatest detail possible, you want to describe exactly what the work of your business is and how it is accomplished.

Now identify why someone would come to you for your product or service instead of going to anyone else who provides the same product or service. What is your distinctive advantage? What makes your business different from others that provide the same product or service? Is your price lower? Is your workmanship superior? Do you offer more or better customer service?

What can you do that others in your industry cannot? What benefits do your competitors promote? What benefits do they fail to promote?

If you have been in business for awhile, look for the answers to these questions:

- What do customers praise you for in their calls or letters?
- How do customers, suppliers, employees describe your company when they tell others about it?

When Lisa Renshaw was twenty-one she started a career outsmarting parking lot owners by proving that she could take over a failing parking lot in a bad part of Baltimore and go against a standard industry operating philosophy — a philosophy that held that people always patronize lots located closest to their destination. Not only did she defy industry standards, but she started her business with only a high school education, no business experience, and the inability to drive a car with a stick shift.

Her first major decision when she became boss of Penn Parking, Inc. (named for the lot's proximity to the Pennsylvania Railroad Station) was to raise parking lot fees. It was her theory that people would park farther away for better service, even if the price was higher. Then, brassy and bold, she passed flyers to commuters as they exited the parking lots of her competitors. Her fliers promised friendlier service and a free car wash for every customer.

Renshaw's success began with fifteen cars per day. She

had one employee who worked days while she took the swing shift from 5:30 p.m. to 1:00 am. Twice she was accosted by muggers, and she chased burglars away, driving after them in her car. She slept on a piece of carpet, barricaded in her office.

Determination and courteous service paid off. Eventually, she landed profitable parking contracts from property owners, and eventually opened four lots which gross more than one million a year. As she learned, people pay extra for courtesy and fair treatment, her distinctive advantages.

Source of capital

If you are just embarking on your business venture, how will you fund your start up and operational costs until the business can generate enough revenue to become self-sustaining? How much capital will it take to get your business off the ground? How much to sustain operations? These are questions you worked through in Chapter Four, "Assessing the Risk." Insert the results of that assessment behind the "Where Are We Right Now" divider. Be sure to review them for accuracy and completeness.

And here is a suggestion. Whatever you anticipate your costs to be, multiply that figure by at least 150 percent. I'm pretty sure that the infamous Murphy wrote a law that covers this: everything costs more than you think it will. Remember that undercapitalization is usually a symptom of a failing business, not the reason for failure. The cause may be poor anticipation of the financial needs of the business, poor planning for success, or poor management of resources.

At this point you will prepare a balance sheet for your

business. Your balance sheet lists assets, liabilities and equity of the business. Total assets must equal liabilities plus
owner equity. In Chapter Nine there will be a discussion of
the critical financial tools that you will need to operate a
successful business. At this point, let me forewarn you that
if you want your business to succeed, you must have a basic
understanding of business finance. If you don't feel comfortable about your current level of understanding, begin
researching how you can attain the expertise you will need
to monitor the financial health of your business. Check with
community colleges, your local Chamber of Commerce,
Small Business Development Corporation (SBDC) programs, or your accountant. Organizations like the American
Management Association have correspondence courses. My
number one recommended financial management book for
small business owners is Bottom Line Basics by Robert J.
Low (see Chapter Ten).

   If you do not acquire the skills necessary to monitor the
financial well-being of your business, you will leave yourself vulnerable to potential disasters. You will read about
some of those disasters in Chapter Ten. In the meantime, if
you need to strengthen your skills, begin researching
resources.

Strengths

   The next four categories comprise what business text
books call a S.W.O.T. analysis — strengths, weaknesses,
opportunities and threats. Personally, I think this is one of
the most exciting phases of strategic planning. You are
going take a more analytic look at the information you gathered about the resources listed in the Where We Are Today
section: people, facilities/equipment, operations and source

of capital. What strengths do you see in these resources? Are the people who are involved enthusiastic, energetic, creative, wise, highly committed, motivated to succeed? Is the location of your facility especially conducive to providing fast, easy turnaround and delivery? Do you have state-of-the-art equipment? When you review all your resources, which ones provide you with the greatest advantages? List them, and if possible, prioritize them.

Weaknesses

Now do the same type of analysis of your resources to find your Achilles heel. Address these weaknesses up front. You will do yourself no favor by minimizing them or denying their existence. Perfection is a myth — we all have weaknesses. What are the weaknesses of your resources?

Opportunities

A considerable portion of the discussion of your opportunities will focus on the market. After all, you are in business to fill a need of consumers, and to be profitable in the process. It doesn't make a lot of sense to start a business without identifying who will be the consumers of its products or services. Among other things you will want to discover is how your anticipated customers are currently having their needs met. Is there an opportunity for you to provide a better quality product or service, or to make it more convenient and/or less expensive for consumers to get their needs met?

If you wanted to open a shoe repair shop, why would you consider locating it on a block where there were already two shoe repair shops unless your business could be distinguished from the others, and unless your shop addressed an opportunity that the other repair shops were missing? One of the existing shops may only be open from 8 a.m. until 5 p.m. Monday through Friday. Could there be an opportunity for you to capture the market of those who work and need to drop off and pick up their shoes between the hours of 6:00 and 7:30 a.m., or 5:30 to 7:00 p.m. or on weekends? The second shop may be equipped with outdated equipment and have to charge prices that are considerably higher than the prices you would have to charge, because your state-of-the-art equipment allows you to make repairs in half the time. Could you offer to repair shoes while customers wait? Is there an opportunity for you to capture the price-and time-sensitive markets?

What are your opportunities for growth and expansion? Is the population of your target market growing? For instance, if you happen to have a product or service that appeals to senior citizens, you could be perched on the brink of exploding sales as baby boomers approach retirement age. What other target markets can you identify that you may move into as your company grows? What opportunities exist because of your resources? Do you have inventors on your staff? Is your equipment flexible enough to easily convert to the production of similar products in the future?

Success magazine published an article about insurance industry innovator Art Williams, who drew on his personal history to see an opportunity for a way of providing improved service to the insurance buying market: "When Art Williams started his own insurance company he certainly did not expect the low-handed maneuvers from competitors that all but stopped his success. His philosophy was striking at the root nerve of the industry — its pocketbook. Insurance giants denounced him in the press as a 'cult' leader. His wife and children endured stares, taunts, and whispers. Agents working for Williams' company, ALW, found their tires slashed and their mailboxes blown up. Bills were introduced in an effort to regulate ALW to death. Underwriters pulled out, forcing Williams to scrounge for backers. But they couldn't stop Williams from turning the insurance industry upside-down, and making insurance policies more buyer-friendly.

"Back when Williams was a junior in college, his father died under-insured, leaving his mother penniless. His father had a typical 'cash-value' policy: a death benefit and a savings plan returning about 1.25 percent, for a premium (in today's money) of $1,000 a year. Williams calls it a 'rip-off.'

"It haunted him for years, especially when hard times found him selling insurance for extra cash. 'Insurance agents like to sell cash-value policies because they return the biggest profit,' says Williams. 'Meanwhile, half of all widows are left destitute.' But a $150,000 term insurance policy typically costs only $200 a year, and includes only death benefits. Williams recommends his customers invest the $800 they save in an IRA or bank account. His motto: 'Buy term, and invest the rest.'"

Art Williams's business grew because he saw an opportunity in the marketplace — an opportunity that addressed a very authentic consumer need — affordable life insurance.

Threats

Analysis of threats usually begins with a look at the competition. It is important to recognize that competition doesn't just come from businesses that offer the same product or service as yours. Competition comes from any business that contends for your customers' dollars. If you are opening a movie theater, other movie theaters are certainly your competition. In addition, live theater, symphonies, operas, and concerts are competition. Furthermore, any business that offers leisure time activities may be competition — video rental stores, bookstores, bowling alleys, miniature golf courses, to name just a few.

What is happening in your target market that may affect the need for your product or service? The timber and fishing industries used to contribute enormously to the economy of the Pacific Northwest. But in the last decade, both have declined substantially. Not only has there been a direct effect on companies in these industries, but also, the companies that manufacture the equipment used in these industries have been heavily impacted by their decline. Is there a weakness in your market? You will want to be sure to study your market carefully and to read all the current information available about it. Check your local library for The Popcorn Report: Faith Popcorn on the Future of Your Company, Your World, Your Life. Although this book was published in 1992, there is much valid information to help you understand current trends in the marketplace.

Consider carefully threats that are specific to your industry, e.g., for a business that manufactures novelty merchandise, it would be especially important to recognize the relatively short life of these types of products. Hula hoops came and went, as did pet rocks, Cabbage Patch Kids and big wheels. Lots of money was made by the companies that manufactured these products — but not for long.

Where Do We Want to Go?

This is where your creative juices will begin to bubble.

Reread the vision statement for your business to rekindle the passion you have for building a successful venture. Then begin putting your pen to paper to examine queries like these:

- What level of sales do you want to achieve this year? Next year? After three years? After five years? After ten years? Will you need to hire additional sales staff? How will you compensate them?
- What gross margin do you project? Will the margin be the same for all products or services, or will it be variable? What percentage of gross profit will you aim to restrict your expenses to? What is your targeted rate of net profit?
- What benefits will your company provide for you and employees in three, five and ten years? Insurance, retirement, employee ownership plan, etc.?
- What new services or new products do you plan to introduce? At what point in time?
- Where will your business be located in three, five and ten years?
- Who will be involved in the business in three, five and ten years? Create organization charts to reflect projected changes in staffing.
- How will your target market change in three, five and ten years?

Every business can benefit from a thoughtful approach to strategic planning. Define success in terms of the results you expect to achieve, identify the customers and their needs, build the internal processes to satisfy those customers, and provide the learning and growth necessary for employees to make a quantum leap in performance. This

process is good common sense. Give thorough consideration to all aspects of your business, and write very specific
goals. "The juxtaposition of vision (what we want) and a
clear picture of current reality (where we are relative to
what we want) generates what we call 'creative tension'; a
force to bring them together, caused by the natural tendency of tension to seek resolution," observes Peter Senge in
The Fifth Discipline.

Four decades ago Florence Chadwick decided she wanted to be the first woman to swim across the English
Channel. She trained diligently, pushing herself to extraordinary limits. Finally, in 1953, the day she dreamed of
arrived. She set out with her mother and trainer in a boat
beside her. Unfortunately, the weather turned stormy as she
approached the coast of England. A heavy, blinding fog
blanketed the water, which in turn became extremely cold
and choppy. Florence valiantly struggled on, until finally, in
desperation and defeat, she asked to be pulled into the boat.
Imagine her disappointment when she found out she had
quit only a few hundred yards from her goal.

Florence told reporters, "I'm not offering excuses, but I
think I could have made it if I had been able to see my goal."
She made up her mind she would try again. This time, while
she continued her demanding physical training, she also
undertook the challenge of memorizing and visualizing the
coastline of England. She created a clear picture of every
feature of the coast in her mind. Finally, she was ready to try
again. And again, just as in her first attempt, the weather
turned bad. The water was churning and the fog blinding.
But this time, Florence, with a clear picture of the coastline
in her mind, made it to the goal.

Visualize and memorize your goals, just as Florence
memorized the English coastline. In Chapter Seven you will

find a format for writing your goals (Goal Setting Worksheet). Use it or create your own format. Notice that the sample worksheet provides for setting goals in each of the four major areas of your business — operations, sales and marketing, finance and ownership. It is easy to become focused on only one area of business development, frequently either operations or marketing. Since most business owners are highly skilled at doing the work of their businesses, they feel very comfortable in the realm of operations. And there is so much focus on marketing in books and magazine articles written for small business owners, that it is easy to find help in establishing specific, small steps for reaching and keeping customers. In my experience, most small business owners feel the least comfortable in the realm of finance and ownership. Goals in the financial area are usually for increased gross revenue and increased net profit. In fact, increased revenue is the result of achieving marketing and sales goals, and increased net profit is the result of attaining other financial goals, such as reducing the cost of goods sold, reducing expenses, etc. And many business owners fail to establish any goals for the ownership function.

See if you can establish at least twelve goals to be achieved by the end of the year and spread them as evenly as possible across the four areas of your business. Next see if you can establish an additional sixteen to twenty goals to achieve by the end of each of your third, fifth and tenth years. The idea is to be realistic while creating a stretch and a policy of continuous improvement for your business. Revisit your goals on a regular basis — the more often the better. You may revamp them at any point in time. But do not place them on a shelf believing that, once you have them written, you are done with them. Successful owners start the engines of their businesses every morning with a review of where they are going.

You may desire to create a lifestyle business, with no aspirations for sustaining a significant growth rate. Be sure you factor in at least enough growth to keep ahead of inflation when you set your revenue goals. You may want to concentrate your goal setting in areas of improving customer service, customer retention, or quality of product and service.

How Will We Get There?

In 1913 Clarence Crane, a candy manufacturer in Cleveland, Ohio, was experiencing a major difficulty in marketing his product. The chocolates he made didn't travel well in the summer months. Orders dropped off drastically — candy stores couldn't sell melted chocolate. If he was to stay in business Crane would have to develop a line of heat tolerant candies. Hard mints might do the trick. Since his factory was set up to produce chocolates only, he outsourced the production of the mints to a pill manufacturer. As luck would have it, the pill maker's equipment was malfunctioning and the whole first batch of mints came off the line flawed. The pill maker apologized to Crane and assured him he would correct the problem, but a light went on for Crane and he said, "No, no, don't fix the problem." The little mints looked like life savers. The flaw was a hole punched in the center of every mint.

But that's not the end of the story. Edward John Noble, who sold advertising space on streetcars in New York City, saw a potential customer for his business when he purchased his first roll of the little mints one day in a candy store. Noble was an eager salesman, but more than that, he was so impressed with the product that he hopped on a train to Cleveland to convince Crane to buy streetcar ads promoting Life Savers. Crane wasn't interested — the mints were simply a sideline to his chocolates. But the zealous Noble persisted, and by the time he returned to New York City he had purchased the Life Saver brand for five thousand dollars.

Noble manufactured and distributed the mints to local candy stores, but sales were slow. He tried giving away free samples on street corners, to no avail. And then he hit upon a brilliant strategy, one that would become a standard in merchandising. He moved the mints out of candy stores and into drug stores, smoke shops, barber shops, restaurants and saloons. He asked each proprietor to place the display of Life Savers near the cash register with a big "5¢" sign, and then to be sure that every customer got a nickel back as part of his change. The strategy worked. Since 1913 the company has sold over fifty billion of the familiar little tubular rolls of candy.

How will you turn your dream into reality? Get your creative juices flowing. Brainstorm with family, friends and associates. See if you can think of twenty, thirty, forty ways to reach each goal, no matter how ridiculous those techniques may seem to you. You can always discard the outrageous suggestions later. But you don't want to stifle the creative process by putting the brakes on during a brainstorming session. You never know what perfectly reasonable strategy may ultimately emerge from a flamboyant, extravagant, unreasonable idea. Up to now, you have concentrated on setting goals for your business. Now it's time to develop the strategies that will enable you to achieve those goals. This is the time, more than any other, when you will want to enlist help. If there are others involved in your business, they are the natural choices for strategizing. We know from research that the more involvement people have in decisions that affect them, the more committed they will be to the successful implementation of those decisions. We also know that when people are left out of decisions that affect them, they may be more than just apathetic about outcomes — they may resort to sabotage so that desired outcomes are not achieved. So if you have associates or employees, involve them as much as is prudent in designing your company's approaches to achieving its goals.

If you are in business alone, you face a greater challenge in finding help to develop your strategies. You may have a family member or friend who heartily supports your endeavor and who would love to help you succeed. If not, have you had a close working relationship with someone whose counsel you value, perhaps in a job or in a volunteer organization? Do you know another small business owner who has been successful for several years? If you buy the pizza and drinks (I recommend sodas — it's good to keep a clear head while you are brainstorming), would a couple of these people be willing to spend a few hours kicking around some possible tactics? And would they be willing to do it on several occasions, until you get your strategies hammered out? After the work is done, you may want to reward them with something more than pizza and sodas! The celebration is important if you feel that you work well together as a team. Eventually, you may want to ask these same people to be your advisors as you build your business. You'll read more about this in Chapter Eleven.

When you get together with your associates, employees, or advisors bring copies of your goals. Your assignment is to determine how you will reach each of your goals, and what benchmarks will indicate your progress en route. You may want to tape sheets of butcher paper to the walls, with one goal written at the top of each sheet of paper. Under each goal, create two columns. In the first column write all the ideas generated for reaching that goal. In the other column write the benchmarks you will encounter as you apply each tactic. These benchmarks will be essential to the measurement of your progress. There will be more about measuring progress in Chapter Eight.

During the course of your brainstorming session, you may realize that you missed writing some important goals. No problem — you can add or subtract goals anytime you want. Your strategic plan is a living, dynamic tool whose purpose is to guide your business along the path to success.

After you are comfortable that you have thoroughly addressed your goals, and formulated reasonable strategies for reaching those goals, transfer your work to a form similar to the one provided in Chapter Seven (Strategic Planning Worksheet).

How Much Will It Cost
To Get Where We Want to Go?

It is probable that as you were brainstorming ideas for achieving your goals, you discarded some because you knew that they were not financially reasonable, sort of a natural selection process. So you already have an approximate idea of how much it will cost to implement each of your strategies. Now it is time to put your research hat back on so that you can determine as precisely as possible what it will actually cost to reach your goals using the strategies you have developed.

If you need to contact vendors of certain goods or services, here are a few tips:

- Contact at least three vendors for each major item you want to price

- Supply all vendors with the most complete, precise specifications list you can produce and with your most precise annual usage estimate
- Ask vendors to submit written bids with the expiration date of the bid and with terms/conditions of sale.
- Maintain a permanent file of all bids received
- Remember to multiply your estimated costs by 150 percent.

Now it's time to get out your calculator and put your pencil to the paper. You are going to create financial projections for your business. You will want to have monthly projections for your first full year in business. Then create annual projections for years one, three, five and ten.

First, how many sales do you expect to make? And how much revenue will be generated by these sales? What do you anticipate your gross profit margin will be on each product or service you sell? Use the information you discovered while researching the costs associated with implementing your strategies. Also draw on the information you acquired during your feasibility study. I hope some of the businesses you visited felt comfortable sharing financial data with you. The data you gathered when researching the Robert Morris Associates' Annual Statement Studies will also help you construct reasonable estimates of gross and net profitability.

Finally, any information that is available regarding predictions for the future of the economy should also be considered. Although predicting the economy is a little like predicting the weather, you might be wise to create three sets of projections: best case, worst case and most likely case. Should the economy turn down, what is the worst impact it would have on your business? If your start up operation should be wildly successful, what would that mean to the financial situation of your business? Somewhere between these two extremes is the prediction of the most likely financial picture.

Your financial projections should answer such questions as: Will you need to borrow money? Will you need to establish a line of credit to supplement cash flow at times? If yes, when, and how much money will you need? You may even want to create a graph of your cash flow forecast so that you can visually depict your tight cash periods and determine how much money you will require to get to the next inflow of cash. What are the projected gross profit margins for each product or service you offer? How will they fluctuate over time, e.g., will volume discounts from suppliers increase your gross profit margin over time?

Finally, be sure to prepare a list of the assumptions you have made in the process of preparing your financial projections. Your assumption list tells anyone reading your projections the reasoning behind your predictions. Without that information, it will be difficult, if not impossible, for your CPA or banker to make sense of your projections. For your initial projections, it is probably wise to footnote every line item, indicating how the estimate was derived.

Later, when you compare your actual numbers with your projections, you will want to review your assumptions to evaluate the differences in the two sets of numbers. This process will greatly improve your knowledge of your business, and your managerial skills.

At the end of Chapter Ten, "Watch the Bottom Line," is a sample income statement. It is intended only to give you a format for your projections, not to dictate the categories you will use for your business. Don't be alarmed when you see that these projections do not call for profitability until after the third year in business. That is not uncommon. You will see that there is substantial interest expense. The projected net loss for the first three years indicates the need to borrow enough money to finance start up costs and interest expense until the company can realize a net profit. (Remember, start up costs are rarely financed by banks. Most start up businesses are financed by their founders.)

If you have a strong accounting or financial background, you may feel confident about your ability to prepare financial projections. But if you are a little wobbly in the knees, be sure to consult an advisor. In many communities help is available through the Small Business Development Corporation (SBDC) offices or Service Corps of Retired Executives (SCORE).

Who Will Do the Work to Get Us There?

Now the challenge is to review the people resources of your company to determine who will be accountable for implementing the strategies and achieving the goals. Remember when you identified the skills and attributes of everyone associated with your business? Use that information to determine who is best qualified to implement each of the strategies. Since we already know that being involved in decisions that concern us results in greater commitment to our efforts, you may want to involve associates and employees as much as possible when assigning accountability.

You're Well On Your Way

When you have finished preparing your written strategic plan, you will very possibly be filled with mixed emotions. On the one hand you may feel drained by the exhaustive research and creative planning you have done. But on the other hand, there are probably feelings of enormous pride and accomplishment. You have done a monumental job of assessing all aspects of your business, and have emerged extremely knowledgeable about that business.

Each one of us has personal resources — often untested — that can sustain and advance our lives, especially in times of transition. You don't need to be more, have more, or know more to tap into this reservoir or to use it to your advantage. You can begin right where you are now chronologically, emotionally and materially. Right now you can begin to make your life work better by capitalizing on the resources you already have at hand. You can build a successful business; you have envisioned exactly what you want your business to look like, you believe that you can achieve that vision, and you have created a plan that will serve as the skeleton around which you will form your business.

Now implementation of your plan lies ahead. Franklin Roosevelt once said, "It is common sense to take a method and try it. If it fails, admit it frankly and try another. But above all, try something."

Once your plan is written, it must be communicated to all employees. Once shared, the plan becomes a unifying force because it reflects the company's values and goals, and how it intends to reach those goals. You are now well prepared to embark upon the next phase of your journey — doing the work of the owner!

7

The Strategic Planning Process

For your convenience, I have chosen to place in one chapter the forms you'll need for recording the information required for the Strategic Planning Process. If you prefer not to write on the pages provided, simply machine copy them and place them in your workbook as a ready reference and resource.

Research and Clarify Where We Are Right Now

1. Identify the people involved in the business (owners/associates/employees): _____

_____
_____
_____
_____

2. Prepare an organization chart for the four basic
   functions of your business (if you are the only person
   involved in your business, your name goes in each
   box on the chart):

```
                    ┌─────────────────┐
                    │     Owner       │
                    │ ─────────────── │
                    └─────────────────┘

┌───────────────┐   ┌───────────────┐   ┌───────────────┐
│ VP Operations │   │  VP Finance   │   │ VP Sales/Mkg  │
│ ───────────── │   │ ───────────── │   │ ───────────── │
└───────────────┘   └───────────────┘   └───────────────┘
```

3. List the skills, experience, and expertise required for
   each of these functions:_____
   _____
   _____
   _____
   _____

4. Evaluate the skills, experience and expertise of every
   person associated with your business: _____
   _____
   _____
   _____
   _____

5. List the facilities and equipment of the business
   (where does the business reside? owned or leased?
   terms of lease? specialized equipment? owned or
   leased? terms of lease? unique capabilities of facilities or equipment?):_____
   _____
   _____
   _____
   _____

6. Explain the operations of your business (product(s)/

service(s) offered? what problem is solved by your
product or service? what's unique? what's your
distinctive advantage? how does work proceed from
order intake to delivery?): _____

_____
_____
_____
_____

7. List your source(s) of capital (remember, undercapitalization is usually a symptom of a failing business,
   not the reason for failure): _____

_____
_____
_____
_____

8. Prepare and attach a balance sheet for your business.

Prepare a Strengths-Weaknesses-Opportunities-Threats (S.W.O.T.) Analysis

9. List your strengths (people, facilities, equipment,
   operations and sources of capital): _____

_____
_____
_____
_____

10. List your weaknesses (address these up front — you
    do yourself no favor by minimizing or denying their
    existence): _____

_____
_____
_____
_____
_____

11. List opportunities you can capitalize on:_____

_____

_____

_____

12. List any existing threats to your venture (competition, technological progress, etc.): _____

_____

_____

_____

Goal Setting Worksheet

Ownership

	Goal	Target Date
#1		
#2		
#3		
#4		

Operations

	Goal	Target Date
#1		
#2		
#3		
#4		

Sales and Marketing

	Goal	Target Date
#1		
#2		
#3		
#4		

Finance

	Goal	Target Date
#1		
#2		
#3		
#4		

Strategic Planning Worksheet
Ownership* Goals
*(*Create a separate worksheet for the goals in each function of your business development)*

Goal	Target Date	Strategies	Benchmark	Accountability
		List all the strategies you will implement to achieve this goal • • • • •	*List the measurements you will use to determine goal has been achieved* • • •	*Who will be accountable for achieving this goal*
Goal #1:				
Goal #2:				
Goal #3:				
Goal #4:				
Goal #5:				
Goal #6:				

Planning to Succeed

Action Item Worksheet

Goal: *(Specific, results-based goal)*

Strategy	Action Items	Estimated Time	Due Date	Done!
#1 *(List each strategy you will inplement)*	1. *(List each step you will take in implementing the*	*How long*	/ /	
	2. *strategy)*	*do you*	/ /	
	3	*think each*	/ /	
	4	*action item*	/ /	
	5	*will take?*	/ /	
	6		/ /	
	7		/ /	
	8		/ /	
#2	1		/ /	
	2		/ /	
	3		/ /	
	4		/ /	
	5		/ /	
	6		/ /	
	7		/ /	
	8		/ /	
#3	1		/ /	
	2		/ /	
	3		/ /	
	4		/ /	
	5		/ /	
	6		/ /	
	7		/ /·	
	8		/ /	
#4	1		/ /	
	2		/ /	
	3		/ /	
	4		/ /	
	5		/ /	
	6		/ /	
	7		/ /	
	8		/ /	
	9		/ /	
	10		/ /	

8

The Work of the Business Owner

Without a doubt, one of the most difficult tasks facing any business owner is setting aside time every day to work on managing and building the enterprise. The operations work of the business has to be done. Customer inquiries need to be handled. Telephone calls and visits interrupt even the most determined. "Fires" have a way of springing up from nowhere! However, there is an unwritten rule that says the number of fires you have to fight each day is inversely proportionate to the number of minutes you spend doing the work of the business owner. In other words, the more time you spend in planning, developing systems, getting help from advisors and coaches, and measuring and monitoring results, the less time you will have to spend taking care of things that don't work the way they should.

Benjamin Franklin was notorious for his understanding of the value of making time to do the work of the business owner. You may recall that he was quoted as saying, "Waste neither time nor money, but make the best use of both." I love this story about Ben: One day he was busy working in the back of his bookstore when a customer stopped in and spent an hour browsing over the various books for sale. Finally, the customer took a book in his hand and asked the shop assistant how much it cost. The assistant replied, "One dollar." The customer, eager for a bargain, said, "A dollar. Couldn't you sell it for less?" But the clerk persisted. "No, the price is a dollar." At that reply, the customer requested to see Mr. Franklin. When Ben appeared from the back room, the customer pressed him for the same information — how much did he want for the book? Without pause, Franklin said, "One dollar and a quarter." The customer was taken by surprise: "Your assistant only asked for a dollar." Franklin said, "If you had bought it from him, I could sell it to you for a dollar. But you have taken me away from the business I was engaged in." The customer persevered, "Come on, Mr. Franklin, what is the lowest price you can take for the book." Now Franklin replied, "One dollar and a half. And the longer we discuss it, the more of my time you are taking and the more I'll have to charge you." Ben understood that to the business owner, time is money!

One of the most important responsibilities of the business owner is to determine which activities are critical to the success of the business. That responsibility is more burdensome for those business owners who have associates and/or employees. For one thing, the owner has an opportunity to be a role model who demonstrates the value of discriminating between essential and non-essential activities and then prioritizing those that are fundamental. In addition, the wise owner understands how important it is to train employees to be prudent in their use of time. It is easier and costs much less to educate, than to be caught in the spiral of hiring and firing. And finally, while successful owners encourage employees to be self-directed and develop independence, they do not leave them without guidance. Instead, they make time to observe each employee's performance and to provide direction when needed. By doing these things, the owner becomes a leader who can exert positive influence to ensure that the work of the business is done efficiently.

Bob Fifer says in Double Your Profits, "Just as there are strategic and non-strategic costs, there is strategic and non-strategic time:

"Strategic time is defined as anything you do that produces profits.

"Non-strategic time is defined as that which is busy and succumbs to the requirements of processes, but which does not contribute to profits.

"Your role as a superlative leader is to communicate by your every action and every utterance that the former is appreciated and the latter is frowned upon. If you change the way you manage your own time and encourage those around you to do the same, you'll see myriad changed behaviors by the people up and down the organization who look to leadership for signals as to what to do."

According to a June 1997 article in Success magazine entitled "The Self-Made Woman," Pamela Lopker's net worth reach $425 million last year. She started her software company, QAD, in 1980 with only $2,000 in start up funds after she quit her job as a software designer. Her niche, she decided, was to create specialized software for manufacturers of specific products. Her niche has served her well. "For each of the last five years, the company's sales have increased by at least 40 percent."

"Lopker says she stays focused by getting up at 5:30 A.M. to run, walk, or go to the gym. 'You can allow yourself to be bogged down with people trying to sell you stuff, interruptions, phone calls,' she says. 'It almost seems as if some things you have to deal with, like sales tax, are set up to tear you down and pull you apart. Every day I have to sit down and say, What do I have to accomplish for this business? You can't let things get you down.'"

It seems as if most everyone these days carries a calendar to record meetings and appointments. What kinds of things do you write on your calendar? If you answered "appointments and meetings," do you generally keep those appointments? Most people respond yes. When an invitation arrives that conflicts with a scheduled appointment, you probably have no trouble declining. Yet you may feel guilty about refusing invitations that only interrupt your usual work, even when that work is critical to achieving your goals.

Here's a surefire suggestion for accomplishing the work of the owner. On your engagement calendar, block out appointments with yourself to do the work of the business owner. Schedule time for planning, developing systems, reviewing financials, getting help from advisors and coaches, and measuring progress toward goals. Hold those dates with yourself as sacred. This can be one of the most powerful tools available to you to overcome the natural tendency to get caught up in fire fighting. Begin today blocking out parcels of time for learning and doing the work of the business owner. Then when an invitation arrives for something that would prevent you from attaining your goal, truthfully say, "I'm sorry, I have an appointment."

Acquiring the skills of the business owner doesn't happen overnight. One cannot just run down to the hardware store and purchase ready-made, one-size-fits-all tools. Nor can one run to the local bookstore and load up on the latest "quick fix" management literature. It takes diligence and hard work to acquire the knowledge and develop the skills necessary to be a professional business owner. People who are serious about building a successful business hit the books, studying subjects like accounting, finance, marketing and production management. They read current periodicals, such as The Wall Street Journal and Fortune, Forbes, Inc., Entrepreneur and Success magazines. Then they apply the sound management principles they have acquired through their studies to their own situations.

Successful business owners realize that they cannot open the doors of their businesses, and then hide inside ignoring the greater community. They keep up on developments in their local business communities by maintaining memberships and being active participants in organizations like the Chamber of Commerce, Rotary, Kiwanis, Lions, etc. They also read local periodicals, publications like The Daily Journal of Commerce, The Business Journal and the daily newspaper. They build networks and alliances with other professionals in their communities, and they are as committed to the prosperity of their friends and colleagues as they are to their own success.

Plan Your Work and Work Your Plan

You may have heard or read that statement before. It is as true now as ever, and if you are serious about building a successful business, working your plan must become a central theme in your daily life.

You already have, or soon will create, as comprehensive a strategic plan as possible for building a successful business. It will become to you what a road map is to a brand new long-haul truck driver who transports loads across country. In the beginning, the driver needs to consult the road map at every major junction, to determine which highway to take and to find how many miles it will be from city to city in order to schedule service and rest stops. The map becomes soiled, wrinkled and dog-eared.

Initially, you should consult your strategic plan every time you make a major decision about the development and operation of your venture. Don't let your plan gather cobwebs because you think you've committed it to memory; look at it. Will the outcome of a decision be consistent with your vision and goals? Will it bring your business closer to its financial projections? Remember, your strategic plan is the source of power to drive your business. Plug into it every day!

Remember, too, that a strategic plan is dynamic and living. As you write the initial plan, you cannot possibly foresee how variables like economic, employment and market conditions will fluctuate, how customer demand will change or how suppliers will emerge or disappear. For instance, who knew in 1993 that businesses would soon create web sites on the internet to give potential customers instant access to information about their products and services, and even give them an opportunity to place on-line orders? And you never know when new threats or opportunities will pop up, requiring you to revisit goals.

Let me give you a personal example that illustrates the flexibility of a strategic plan. When I first decided to build a career as a business development coach and consultant, I wrote a strategic plan outlining my goals, the strategies I would implement to achieve them, and the benchmarks that would measure my attainment of those goals. My highest priority goal was enrolling new coaching clients. One of the many strategies for achieving that goal was to become a professional speaker, on the assumption that when business owners heard my message about planning to succeed, some of them would seek a coach to assist them in the successful development of their companies. Some of them would seek me.

Believing that I had an obligation to give a professional, substantial and powerful presentation to the groups that engaged me, I read every book I could find on speaking, sought training from a professional speech coach, and joined the National Speakers' Association (NSA). The local Portland, Oregon chapter of NSA sponsored a workshop, which I attended, about writing a book in order to use the written word to supplement the message of the spoken word. Bookpartners, Inc., the publisher of the book you are reading, contacted me after that workshop to say that they would like to publish my book (though at that point I didn't even have a book). Little did I realize, when I agreed, that I would ecstatically lose myself in this project.

Writing a book is an enormous undertaking. I can vividly recall reaching the point when it consumed so much of my passion and energy that I told my personal coach, Linda, that I was revising my strategic plan. My goals had changed. Writing the book and touring the country to speak about the concepts of building a successful business became my highest priority goals. I still wanted to coach business owners, but time would only permit me to work with the clients I was already coaching.

When this book is published, I plan to spend six months touring the country speaking about it. When the tour is completed, I will once again revise my strategic plan. I will be ready to revisit my set-aside goals or set new goals, and create the strategies for reaching them.

It is important, once you have created your strategic plan, that you establish a goal for using it. Plug into its incredible energy source. Here is a strategy for attaining that goal:

- For one month (or longer if you have a complex plan), reserve the first ten to fifteen minutes of every business day to peruse your plan. If your business is complex, and you have several associates or employees, you may also want to schedule a weekly time for a review with them. Allow the plan to remind you of your goals and your strategies. Review your benchmarks. Create action items if you see a need (see the next section to learn about action items). Verify that you are measuring the progress you make from benchmark to benchmark (a section on measuring follows).
- For the next four to six months, review your plan on a weekly basis.
- Forever after, review your plan monthly. You are going to establish a regular pattern of analyzing the financial soundness of your business at the end of every month (See Chapter Ten).

Make a habit of reviewing your strategic plan at the same time. Today's comprehensive, easy-to-use accounting software packages make a fairly effortless task of comparing actual financial per formance with projected or budgeted figures. However, your strategic plan contains more than just financial goals. There are also the marketing, operations and owner objectives. Review your strategic plan to see how well your performance in these areas compares to your expectations.

List "Strategic Plan Review" on your calendar for the appropriate days. Make it the first item you accomplish at work on those days. For some business owners, this will seem like a time-wasting exercise. Allow me to explain the rationale. It is easy to get caught up in the daily activities of a business; the pressing needs of employees, suppliers and clients scream for attention. And it is equally easy to ignore the things that don't command center stage, things like reviewing the strategic plan. What keeps us doing the little incidentals are habits and systems (See Chapter Nine).

I don't remember how old I was when I began brushing and flossing my own teeth. My parents gave me the tools and showed me how to use them. And then, for days, weeks, months, possibly even years, they reminded me morning and night to brush my teeth until, finally, it became a habit. As a little kid I understood when they told me how important dental hygiene was to maintaining healthy teeth and gums. But I assure you, I found that the pastimes and treasures of childhood commanded my full attention. Without patient reminders from my parents, I would never have developed the twice daily brushing habit that has become an integral part of my life. My teeth and gums would have rotted by the time I was a teenager! Now brushing is such an unconscious activity that I have, on occasion, brushed my teeth twice before going to bed.

Using your strategic plan as a road map is so important to the successful development of your business that it deserves to become a habit. Let your daily calendar assume the role my parents took when they reminded me every day to brush my teeth. Give it a try. You have nothing to lose by implementing this strategy, and a great deal is at stake if you choose not to.

In Double Your Profits, Bob Fifer outlines his time management habits: "The first thing I do in the morning of every work-day is divide everything I have to do that day into three lists. The first list includes anything that brings in new business (i.e., raises revenue) or eliminates costs. (These are the only two ways you can create profit, since profit equals revenue minus cost.) The second list includes things I have to do to maintain existing business or keep an existing internal operating system running. The third list includes all the things that someone expects or wants me to do, but that really add no value to the bottom line. I never start on my second list until I've done everything on my first list, and never start on my third list until I've done everything on my second list. I always get everything on my first list done before noon that day, when my mind is most alert and my mood most constructive. I always get everything on my second list done by mid-afternoon. Sometimes I finish my third list, and sometimes I decide I've had enough, and I go home."

Action Items

The eighth tab in your binder is the one that will get the most use over time. Behind it you will file the actions you are going to take, in fulfillment of your strategies, to accomplish the goals you have created for your company. These are the little steps that one by one move you forward.

Let's say you have set a goal of creating and nurturing a network of contacts. Your strategies are to:

• join one community group and one business organization
• attend meetings regularly and be an actively participating member of both in order to meet new contacts and learn about their businesses.

Here's what often happens to a struggling business owner. She recognizes the value of the goal, and she knows she should implement the strategies — someday, as soon as she can get around to it. Time passes. Driving home from work in the evening, she remembers those good strategies, but with hundreds of things on her mind she forgets about them by the time she drives into her garage. At lunch with friends, she is reminded of her strategies by a passing comment and this time she scribbles a reminder note on a paper napkin and shoves it in her pocketbook. Eventually, the reminder note ends up on her desk, where it is shifted from one pile to another. And sometimes, her strategies actually get implemented. Often they don't.

Successful business owners act to ensure that their strategies are implemented. And to guarantee that they don't forget or procrastinate, they use a system to record the actions they will take, and to check them off once they are taken. There are "canned" systems available in a wide range of formats and prices which are very popular. Some come as diaries or notebooks; some are available as software. There are trade-offs. If you don't have a laptop computer, it is impossible to carry the software versions with you. If you use the diary format, it can't dial phone numbers or send follow-up letters. If you should decide that you want to invest in one of the canned systems, frequently called "contact management systems," use the due diligence skills you learned in Chapter Three to research which one will be the best fit for your needs.

If you don't want to buy a canned system, you can create one with your own sophisticated strategic planning tools, pencil and paper. Let's return to our example of the owner who plans to join and actively participate in one community group and one business organization. What actions might she want to take in order to implement the first strategy? Here is a list of action steps she might take in her quest:

1. Identify community groups

2. Call each group for information

3. Attend one meeting of each group

4. Attend a second meeting of those groups that she considers a good fit

5. Apply for membership to selected group

These are small incremental steps which, when followed, will lead her to the implementation of the first strategy. Each of these action items can be assigned a duration in minutes or hours. That makes it easy for her to plug them into slots on her daily calendar. Have you ever found yourself thinking that you might be wasting time during the day — five minutes here, three minutes there — because there just isn't enough time to start a project? People who use action item lists can almost always find something they need to do that will fill the open slots.

In order to ensure that action items don't remain on the list forever, it's a good idea to date their entry, and possibly to indicate the date by which they must be completed. If there are associates or employees in your business, you may choose to assign an action item to someone else. Be sure to indicate who is accepting accountability for each action item. And finally (this is my favorite part) be sure there is a way to check the item off when it has been completed. At the end of Chapter Seven you will find my suggested prototype for your consideration, although you may think of more creative or sophisticated ways to format your action item list.

Some people choose to use colors to denote levels of importance, or different pages for different types of action items. Create whatever form works best for you, one that you will train yourself to use. It's time again to hear the voice of your parents, reminding you to brush your teeth. In other words, create a system that will train a habit.

As a suggestion, enter two notations on your calendar every day for a month. The first notation will be a reminder to yourself that the last thing you will do every day is go through your list of uncompleted action items. Which ones are critical to the development of your business? Block out time on your calendar to tackle and complete those items first. Also, block out time early in each day to plunge into your most difficult action items. The longer you delay in starting a troublesome project, the bigger it looms. Here is another saying of unknown origin that graces my office wall:

If you've got a frog to swoller, don't look
at him too long before you swoller him.
If you've got two frogs to swoller,
swoller the big one first!

There is a special benefit to doing your hardest tasks first — the feeling of accomplishment one gets after completing a detestable task provides incredible momentum. As Albert Schweitzer said, "One who gains strength by overcoming obstacles possesses the only strength which can overcome adversity."

Prioritize other action items and block out the time on your calendar when you will undertake them. When blocking out time to tackle action items, be realistic. Leave adequate time in your day to receive or return phone calls; open the mail and respond to it; handle inquiries from associates, employees, suppliers and clients; and so on.

The second notation in your calendar will be for the second thing you will do at work every morning (remember the first thing you will do is to review your strategic plan). It will remind you to go through your calendar to refresh your memory about the things you will tackle that day. Be diligent about tackling those items and maintaining your schedule. There will certainly be times when you cannot complete the action items on your calendar. No problem; move them to the next day. The important thing is to train yourself to use a system for accomplishing the critical tasks of the owner.

Measure, Measure, Measure

This is probably the key motivator in keeping your business moving forward. It's easy to get complacent about progress, just showing up at work every day and doing the "stuff" that accumulates there begging for time and attention. Successful business owners refuse to allow themselves to get sucked into the quagmire of status quo. Instead, they are continually aware of the benchmarks they must reach to move their businesses forward and they habitually measure their progress.

Here's a strategy for measuring progress toward your goals. Create a chart and find a place to post it near your desk or workstation. Down the left side of the chart list each of the benchmarks you are going to monitor. To the right of this list create a grid. The columns of the grid are dated one week apart. Reserve a regular weekly time on your calendar when you will monitor progress toward each benchmark. Place a check mark in the appropriate square after you have determined what progress has been made. If you reach a benchmark, paste a gold star in the appropriate square. Some may think this is too much like kindergarten, but I surmise that even adults receive great affirmation and reward when they see the number of stars mounting. This gives us the motivation to continue striving to reach other benchmarks. If you respond positively to this kind of motivational stimulation, create some additional levels of reward. For every five gold stars you paste on your chart, give yourself a special perk.

Those who know me well, and have worked with me over the years, understand that I place great value on visual reminders. My office walls have always been designated as a gallery to display motivational words of wisdom and charts for measuring progress toward goals. In addition, I have been known to wear buttons reading, "Has anyone told you today that you are terrific?" and "No one of us is as great as all of us together." I have created and worn banners (like Miss America's) that are visual reminders of progress toward our goals. All of these visual systems are contrived to create focus. Measure your progress toward your goals every week as a way of maintaining your focus and momentum.

If you have associates or employees, be sure to develop a reward system that includes everyone. Here's a tip: perks and rewards don't have to be elaborate or expensive. The number one reward people want to receive for their contribution at work is recognition! So have fun with your merit system. Use stickers or flowers or beanies to identify and reward achievers. And be sure to have a celebration when you hit an especially significant benchmark, or when you have accumulated lots of gold stars.

Whenever you reach a goal, it's time to start brainstorming about what the next goal will be. Succeeding in business, and maintaining that success, is all about progress. Businesses that fail to acknowledge the change required for progress will stagnate and dwindle. So when you have accomplished what you set out to accomplish, figure out what you need to accomplish next:

- Set a goal
- Determine the strategies you will implement to reach that goal

- Identify the benchmarks that will reveal your progress toward your goal
- Add those benchmarks to your wall chart and begin monitoring progress toward their achievement.

Commit Everything Important to Writing

You may have noticed a theme that runs through this entire book. Commit everything you want to accomplish to writing. The importance of writing your major goals was discussed. For the same reason (that things that are written are committed to and get done) it is important to write down even the little things you want to accomplish: making a phone call, writing a thank you note, buying gold stars for a chart. Create an Action Item for each of them, because that increases the probability that they will get done. Here's what happens to most business owners: our brains get overloaded with information and tasks to be accomplished. Did you know that one of the jobs of your brain is to hang onto your thoughts and ideas until it is given permission to let go of them? I mentioned this fact before, but the process is worth repeating. Do you ever lie awake, or awaken in the middle of the night, with your mind racing? What do you do to get back to sleep? Most people find that they simply need to put their thoughts down on paper, releasing the brain from its responsibility.

My theory is that the brain is like the letter slots behind the front desk of an old-fashioned hotel. Once all the slots are full, if more mail comes in, something has to give. When the new mail is slipped into the slot, the old mail falls out the back of the slot onto the floor. It's still there, it's just harder to reach. If you are committing all the information and tasks of your job (or your life) to memory, something has to give. Although all of the information is still in your brain somewhere, much of it becomes inaccessible.

Take the pressure off your memory. Cultivate a great habit starting now — write everything down. Use your calendar and your Action Items list to keep track of your goals, strategies and benchmarks. A great value-added benefit is that your mind will be gloriously freed to generate and pursue creative ideas.

Financial planning and analysis, systems and procedures development, and seeking advisors and maximizing the value of their input are such important aspects of what the business owner does, that each has been allocated a separate chapter. Together with planning and working the plan, and monitoring and measuring progress, they comprise the work that successful business owners commit to performing on a regular basis to ensure the successful development of their ventures.

Have Fun

Much of the information in this book is serious in nature, but I don't want to forget to encourage a very important part of you, that part with the passion to go into business for the love and fun of it. It is my personal belief that I only get one go-around at life, so it is crucial that I enjoy every minute I have. If I didn't love what I were doing, I would quit doing it and do something else instead. I look at every day as another opportunity to learn, meet new people, stretch and grow.

Part of having fun with your business stems from having a fulfilling life outside of work. In my experience, those owners who have outside interests that are at least as important as their work possess a healthy perspective about the challenges that ownership presents. They come to work with fresh ideas and an abundance of energy.

There was a period of time while I owned my first business (the least successful of three), when it was not uncommon for me to work fourteen to sixteen hours a day, six to seven days a week. I can recall being so tired and drained that I couldn't conceive of a clever idea and made lots of mistakes. In addition, I wasn't a fun person for my children and friends to be around. At some point, I realized that it would be far better for me to practice good self-management, get adequate rest breaks, and cultivate outside interests. It was at that point that my friend Janet and I decided to combine our talents and work together. Our business soared and we began to have a lot of fun.

9

Anything Worth Doing
Is Worth Doing Intentionally
and Systematically

Customers — that's who drives business. There is a worn, but true, maxim that suggests, "It's easier and less expensive to keep the customers you have than to acquire new customers." One of the most powerful ways to keep current customers is to systematize your operations so that clients have the same experience every time they encounter your business. Once again, I refer you to The E Myth Revisited by Michael Gerber. There are powerful anecdotes in that book to convince you of the value of systematizing your operations.

One of the biggest turnoffs for customers is to receive a level of service that is inconsistent with their expectations.

The first time you do business with a customer, you set the level of expectation for the future:

- If the first experience is poor, you may never have an opportunity to change the expectation. The customer will find another supplier.
- If the first experience is good, and subsequent experiences are either better or worse, you confuse and frustrate the customer.
- *A worse experience may be intolerable; several worse experiences surely are intolerable.
- *A better subsequent experience may be favorable, as long as the customer realizes it is better because you are making a conscious, planned effort to improve service (and it will really be favorable if you have surveyed that customer about his past experience and responded to his suggestions for improving future experiences).
- *A better subsequent experience followed by a worse experience (in other words, the customer never knows what kind of service he'll receive) almost always predicts the demise of a business relationship.

So how can you ensure that your customers will receive the same level of service every time they do business with you? By doing several things, which include but are not limited to: designing and documenting your exact procedures for dealing with all aspects of your business; surveying customers to determine their level of satisfaction and their suggestions for improving that satisfaction; continually researching ways that you can improve your customer satisfaction procedures; and finally, making sure customers know that any changes in your service are results of your conscious efforts to improve, not quirks in your system.

By the way, quirks do occur. That is part of our human experience. Never, never, never let them slip by unrecognized or unreconciled. Let your customers know that you are aware your system failed, that you will fix what went wrong, and that you value their business and want to continue serving them in the future.

In her book, *Customer Loyalty*, Jill Griffin recounts this story: "When an American husband and wife purchased a faulty Sony compact disc player at a Tokyo department store, they received a lesson in customer loyalty that completely overwhelmed them and turned their anger into amazement.

"The couple, who were staying with the husband's parents in the outlying city of Sagamihara, had tried to operate the disc player the morning after the purchase and were disappointed when it wouldn't run. Further investigation proved there was no motor or driving mechanism in the case.

"Annoyed and perplexed, the husband had been practicing the scathing denunciation he planned to register by telephone with the manager of the Odakyu Department Store on the dot of 10 a.m. when the store opened.

"But at 9:59 a.m., the phone rang...The caller was none other than Odakyu's vice president, who clamored effusively that he was on his way over with a new disc player.

"In less than an hour, the vice president of the company and a junior employee were standing on the doorstep. The younger man was laden with packages and papers. As they met the customer at the door, both men began bowing enthusiastically.

"Continuing to bow, the younger man began explaining the steps they had taken to rectify their mistakes. On the day the customers had left the store, a salesclerk had discovered the problem and requested security guards to stop them at the door. Since they had already left, the clerk reported the error to his supervisor, who reported to his supervisor, and so on, until the vice president learned of the error. Since the only identification the store personnel had was an American Express card number and name, they began there.

"The clerk called thirty-two hotels in and around Tokyo to ask if the couple was registered. That turned up nothing, so a staff member was asked to stay late at the store, until 9 p.m., when the American Express headquarters in New York would be open. American Express gave him the couple's home phone number. When the employee called that number, at almost midnight Tokyo time, he reached the wife's parents, who were house-sitting. He learned the couple's address in Tokyo from the wife's parents.

"The young employee, breathless from his recitation, then began offering gifts to the customers: a new $280 disc player, a set of towels, a box of cakes, and a Chopin disc. In less than five minutes, the astonished couple watched the vice president of the store and his employee climb back into a taxi — after their profuse apologies for having made the customers wait while the salesclerk rewrote the sales slip. They sincerely hoped the couple would forgive the mistake.

"While most stores would replace defective merchandise, how many would go to such lengths to make an unhappy customer a lifelong buyer?"

Design and Document Procedures

One of the joys of starting your own business is that you can determine exactly how you want to handle all aspects of your ownership, marketing and sales, operations, and finance and accounting functions. When you think about these functions, picture each as part of a bigger system. When you design how each will work, take into consideration how it will interact with the other functions.

The human body is a system with which most people are familiar. It is made up of many smaller systems — respiratory, circulatory, excretory, digestive, nervous, endocrine, etc. None of these systems operates independently. The heart pumps the blood through the lungs where the oxygen-carbon dioxide exchange occurs. The digestive system contributes food to the circulatory system. The digestive system delivers waste products to the excretory system. And so it goes.

Similarly, the work you do to market your business will generate sales. The sales you close will create the work to be done by your operations function, and create accounting entries. Delivering your finished product or service will result in more accounting entries. Before you begin to design the written procedures for doing the work of your business, it is important to look at the overall picture of your business system. How does each function relate to the others? How will you provide the interface between functions?

Some business owners find it helpful to create a flow chart that depicts how the functions of their business relate to one another. This doesn't have to be a fancy document — sometimes the simpler the diagram, the easier it is to grasp the links. By creating the flow chart first, it ensures that no process will be overlooked when procedures are being written.

Once you have determined all the links, examine each function in detail and break it down into the smallest steps, just like you break strategies down to Action Items. All the steps are then committed to writing, and filed in a procedural manual. Create footnotes for steps that are based on assumptions so that you can revisit your reasoning at a later date.

There are two prudent reasons to document procedures for all functions of your business. The first is to create consistency in your product and service. The second is to ensure that someone else could step in and run your business without interruption, because any owner could have an illness or accident that would put her or him out of commission for an extended period of time, or your business could grow to the point that you need to hire someone to do some of the work. Procedural manuals are of inestimable value in training an employee to provide a consistent level of service.

Your procedural manual should not only contain a detailed description of each function, but it should also contain a copy of every form that accompanies that function. The detailed description includes step-by-step, numbered instructions. On the accompanying sample form, corresponding numbers are recorded in the appropriate places. When someone is unsure of how to complete any portion of the form, he or she simply needs to check the written procedures, find the number, and read the instructions.

At the end of this chapter I have provided a sample lead tracking form and the accompanying pages from a sales and marketing procedural manual (see pages XX) which explain how to use the form and how to complete all pertinent processes related to the form.

Procedures vs. Rules

Procedures provide support for your business the way skeletons provide support for our bodies. Just as our skeletons allow our bodies to move and be flexible, the procedures you create for your business should allow you, your associates and your employees to be flexible and responsive to your customers. The challenge is to create procedures, not rules that restrict.

Norm Brodsky writes in "We Have Met the Enemy, and He Is Us," in the June 1997 issue of *Inc.* magazine, "I can understand why companies have rules. Employees have to know where the boundaries lie — how they're supposed to conduct themselves, what's going to get them into trouble and what isn't. Some rules you establish for survival's sake, to avoid mistakes that might put you out of business. Others you have because you want to maintain certain standards. Still others you decide you need after you get whacked on the head. Then there are those you institute because you think you've discovered a terrific new way to boost your sales or streamline your management system or cut your costs— whatever.

"Behind every rule there's almost always a good reason, or at least a good intention. At the time you establish them, the rules appear to make all the sense in the world. And yet, if you're not careful you run a high risk of creating rules that will hurt your business. What happens is that you take away your employees' ability to use common sense in responding to the reasonable requests of customers."

Brodsky explains how his company added a rule about reversing rush charges. As it used to be, when a customer complained about an unfair rush charge any customer service representative had the authority to reverse the charge when justified. But a couple of reps were careless in their evaluation and reversed all late charges, so a new rule was instituted: no reversals of late charges without authorization of management. Consequently, even when customers explained that rush charges were unjustified, customer service reps refused to reverse them, saying, "Well, you'll have to speak to a manager." The managers would subsequently waive the late charges, but only after the customers became enraged at their treatment.

Brodsky continues, "By the time I realized what was happening, my rule had already done some damage. Needless to say, I got rid of it. Now our customer service reps are allowed to decide for themselves whether or not to issue a credit. At times when we're at fault, I hope they do. Will some reps make bad decisions? Probably, but then we'll just have to train them to do better.

"In retrospect, it's obvious I made a mistake by establishing a rule just because a couple of employees were loose with credit. The right response would have been to put in the time and effort required to get them up to speed.

"And that's really the point. We tend to make bad rules not when we're attacking problems but when we're avoiding them. We fall into the trap of looking for shortcuts and easy answers. So one bad customer drives off without paying his bill, and we put restrictions on all our good customers. Or one employee uses poor judgment in issuing credit, and we tie the hands of all those whose judgment is perfectly sound.

"The result is bad customer service."

Survey Customers

There are a number of ways to seek feedback from customers. One is a short, three- to four-item questionnaire which can be printed on a small card. Every prospect or customer who visits your business is asked to complete the card. Let them know that you are always working to improve your customer service. Most people will gladly answer three to four questions. The questions you ask will be determined by your business. You may want to know how they found out about your business, how easy it was to locate your business, how well their needs were met by your product or service, and whether they received friendly and efficient service.

Some business owners choose to focus on one area of their business for a period of time, then change their focus for the next period, i.e. inquire about the quality of product or service, then inquire about packaging and delivery, then ask about efficiency and friendliness of staff, etc. You may choose to leave a blank line for comments on each survey to obtain unsolicited comments. Sometimes customers have things to tell businesses that the owners didn't think of asking about.

Another way to ask customers for information is by enclosing a survey with every invoice. This questionnaire may be longer, because the customer can complete it at home or work. The rate of return for this type of questionnaire may be lower because some customers do not return the survey. There is a trade-off, though. The questionnaires that are returned often contain more in-depth responses.

Recently, a client who is currently undertaking a survey project asked me how long she needed to continue soliciting feedback from her customers. My response took the form of a question: How long does she want customers to keep coming back? How long and how often you survey your customers may depend upon the kind of business you operate. If you have a stable customer base, you may only want to conduct a survey periodically. If you own a retail store, with new customers purchasing from you every day, you may want to survey on a continuing basis.

Sometimes businesses choose to hire a marketing

research company to survey customers and potential customers. These types of surveys are carefully constructed
and should yield very reliable information. The trade-off is
that these surveys are costly. Marketing research companies
are frequently hired to test the market before the introduc-
tion of a new line of products. As part of the due diligence
process, businesses may choose to spend research money
before committing significantly large amounts of capital to
a product that customers don't want or won't buy.

If a small business begins conducting surveys early in its
life, and surveys frequently, it should have a dependable
source of information about customer satisfaction. In addition, surveying customers helps to build the good will that
brings repeat and referral business.

Research Ways to Improve Service

Besides asking your prospects and customers to voice
their opinions, there are several other suggestions for finding ways to improve your service:

- Continually study your industry. Participate in associations, attend conventions, and read publications.
- Visit your competitors and related businesses. What
  systems and procedures can you observe? If you are
  well known by your competitors, have a friend or
  advisor "shop" your competitors. How do your prices,
  service, delivery and quality compare to the competition? Be sure to evaluate the competition at least twice
  a year.
- Be alert to the possibility that the systems and
  procedures you see being used in any business might
  be applied to your business.
- Read, read, read. Read current business books and
  periodicals, everything you can find on how to provide

the best possible service. You may want to start with *Customer Loyalty: How to Earn It, How to Keep It* by Jill Griffin. Whatever your industry, whatever the size of your business, your success depends on building a loyal clientele.

Promote Your Customer Service Improvement System

Be sure to post signs in your business, on your delivery trucks, on your sales brochures and invoices, maybe even in print advertising, that you value customer input and that you implement appropriate, prudent suggestions. You might add a line to your invoices each month acknowledging a person who made a suggestion for improving your product or service.

One word of caution. Some customer suggestions won't work for your business. Be sure you thank every person for his/her input. Let him or her know that you will consider the suggestion in light of all your systems and procedures. Be sure to explain that if you do not implement the suggestion, it may not be a good fit, or the timing might not be right.

Remember to update your procedural manuals whenever you make a change to your business systems. Procedural manuals are an essential part of the successful entrepreneur's tools, and just like the strategic plan, they should be reviewed on a regular basis for accuracy. You want to make sure that you haven't forgotten a procedure you really intend to follow; you also want to make sure that if you have changed the way you do something, your written procedures reflect that change.

Computer Based Systems

It is hard to imagine how most businesses could operate without a computer. Whatever your venture, you may choose to simplify the management of your systems by using one or more computers. Computer hardware becomes increasingly efficient and less expensive all the time. Software is also reasonably priced. Basic business software often includes:

- a word processor
- spreadsheet and database capabilities
- accounting software, including accounts payable, accounts receivable, financial statement and inventory control capacity
- a contact/calendar manager, and
- an internet server.

The glory of computer hardware and software is that systems designers and programmers have already done the work of interfacing processes. The business owner needs to install the software, learn how to use it, teach employees how to use it, and monitor the outcome.

Some businesses need to have software written specifically for their use, or have existing software custom tailored to their needs. This can become fairly expensive, and debugging programs can seem like a nuisance. I know one small business that purchased payroll software that needed to be customized. For over a year they struggled with an incomplete system, frequent breakdowns, and inaccurate information. The information systems manager spent countless nights trying to juggle the nightmarish process. Finally, the company scrapped the software all together and outsourced the payroll preparation.

If you are not comfortable with your ability to maximize

the use of a computer system, you may want to enroll in classes available at community colleges or private computer training companies. You may also want to find a computer consultant who will be available to help you if you run into problems you cannot correct by reading manuals or calling for technical support (both come with computer hardware and software).

One of the pitfalls of relying on computers is the devastating effect that loss of the equipment can have. My computer is central to my business. When there is a power outage, I lose access to nearly all work in process, information about clients, and my calendar and Action Item list. Power outages are usually brief, so I have reading I can do to fill my down time, and it doesn't take long to get back up and running once the power is restored. Much more devastating is the loss of the computer because of equipment breakdown. I have a wonderful repair company that can often return my computer within a couple of days.

Here is a final word about computers. Be sure to create backup files for your data. I experienced a hard drive "crash" once, and while the technicians were able to salvage some of the data stored there, most was severely compromised. It was necessary to reinstall all the software programs, and to re-load files from backup disks. There are powerful automated systems available that systematically take care of creating backup files when you close your computer for the day.

Networking

One of the most effective, personally satisfying ways to attract customers is through systematic networking. It is vital for humans to network for their common good.

Indigenous people have always understood this. Tribes of people with diverse talents and skills pool their resources for the betterment of the whole. In modern America, networks are our safety net, a matrix of relationships that can buoy us during times of change and offer pathways to business success.

People who regularly keep in touch, and give as much as or more than they get, find that their occasional requests for assistance and advice are welcomed and accommodated. Networking relationships are for the long haul, and are maintained through courteous reciprocity. Building a network is a way of connecting with the wider world, and opening yourself to all its exciting possibilities. John Naisbitt, a futurist and author of the bestseller *Megatrends*, says "Networks are structured to transmit information in a way that is quicker, more energy efficient, more high tech than any process we know." Cookie mogul Wally "Famous" Amos defines networking as "making new friends and maintaining and growing existing relationships."

The theory is that you should be able to reach anyone who could be of help to you in three phone calls. And the good news is that you already have a built-in network of family, friends, and acquaintances:

- Family of origin: parents, siblings, aunts/uncles, cousins
- Family of choice: spouse or partner, children, stepchildren, in-laws
- Friends: high school and college friends — classmates, dorm/roommates,fraternity/sorority associates; neighbors (current and past), church members, support group members
- Business associates (current and past), bosses, colleagues, employees, service club members,

professional association members, customers/clients, suppliers, volunteer organization members
- Advisors and personal services providers: CPA/ financial planners, lawyers, fitness trainers, child care workers, domestic help (housekeeper, landscaper, nanny), therapists, health professionals (doctor, dentist, chiropractor, veterinarian, massage therapist, etc.), religious/spiritual advisors, athletic associates (club, team, etc.)
- Course/lecture/workshop participants and instructors.

To mobilize and expand the effectiveness of your personal support networks:
- Ask for direct help and be receptive when it is offered
- List six people with whom you would like to improve your relationship and at least one action step you will take with each person toward this improvement
- Get rid of relationships that are not supportive or are damaging to you
- Maintain high-quality business relationships by telling people how much you value their support and dedication
- Review your present network, make an honest assessment of how well it is working for you, and identify areas where you could use some changes
- Keep your energy exchange balanced, return favors and thoughtfulness.

Most of us would say that the people we care about make life worth living. They give it meaning and purpose. The quality of relationships makes the difference in our lives at all ages. Human relationships are critical for the normal functioning of our personalities. The need for interaction with other people is built into the very essence of human nature. The good times are better because we can share them. The bad times are less painful because we can share them. Change is easier because we can usually rely on other people for support if they understand the reasons for our change.

Know who can help you make intelligent changes in your life (friends, peers, family members, colleagues, professional advisors help reduce stress at times of change). Develop a network, a team of people, in order to avoid being dependent upon one or two people, or getting advice and information from limited sources. Our relationships provide opportunities for personal change, deepening our understanding of ourselves, reinforcing our competence, and championing our belief in our ability to achieve our goals. Because none of us is as smart as all of us together, set up your relationships so that you can call upon the collective "brain trust," or your network, in time of need.

Art Berg knows about the personal cost of painful change, and he knows the value of having friends to support you when traditional companies write you off as a cripple whose contributions are questionable. Art's story, published in *Success* magazine, pictured him at twenty-one as a bright young entrepreneur with a sweetheart and a prosperous tennis court construction company.

"While driving him to the wedding, Art Berg's friend nodded off at the wheel, and the car crashed into an embankment. Berg was thrown from the mass of twisted metal and hurled against the ground.

"Berg was almost completely paralyzed, and his doctors advised him he would never get another job. And indeed, when he tried to run his company from his hospital bed, he was too weak and had to let the company go.

"'An agency for disabled people tried to place me in a job,' says Berg. 'But they said, "Forget sales." They said people wouldn't want me around, that I'd be better off answering phones.'

"Doctors, psychiatrists, and career advisors urged Berg to face the truth: His career and normal life were over. The sooner he accepted that, the better off he would be.

"But one thought echoed in his head, an idea he'd read in a book by Napoleon Hill: Nothing bad ever happens without equal or greater benefit in return.

"'I decided this could be the greatest experience of my life,' says Berg.

"Berg's dream was to sell products. 'I understood employers felt at risk. So I told them that if I didn't outsell their top producer in thirty days, I'd leave, and they didn't have to pay me anything.'

"Numerous companies passed on Berg's offer — until Bell Atlantic hired him. In three years there, he won three national awards for sales excellence. Berg and his fiancée married and moved to Utah, where he opened several book-stores, with sales surpassing half-a-million dollars within a year. In 1992, he was named regional Young Entrepreneur of the Year.

"Berg wrote his own book, *Some Miracles Take Time*, which sold more than 20,000 copies, and started Invictus Communications Inc. in Provo, Utah, to manage his public speaking. It is not unusual for him to travel 180,000 miles and speak to 150 different groups in a year. Always a topic in his speeches is the value of networking.

"Berg has also become a world-class wheelchair athlete — scuba diver, parasailer, and tennis player. And every morning, he wakes up full of hope that this will be the day he'll walk again.

"'Pain comes to teach us,' Berg says, 'If we become frustrated, we lose the lesson. When we see pain as having a purpose in life, it drives us closer to our dreams.'"

Art Berg was able to build a fulfilling and productive life after his accident with the support and help of the people in his network. Take a lesson from Art Berg: As you add advisors and professionals to your network, ask yourself:

• Does this person have the experience with this business issue to help me?

   • Has this person consistently demonstrated concern for my best interests?

   • Does this person share my value system? Does he/she want the same result for my business that I do?

   • Is this person trustworthy with confidential information?

Systems Only Work If You Use Them

One of my favorite books is *Endless Referrals*, by Bob Burg. It's a favorite, because Burg shares powerful systems for building a successful business by helping others succeed — the very core of successful networking. In the last chapter of his book, he reminds us of something that should be obvious. "Throughout this book you've been exposed to techniques that can and will account for a dramatic increase in both your personal happiness and financial earnings, but only if you take the information and apply it!

"How often has it been noted that knowledge without action is the same as having no knowledge at all? To succeed in your quest for endless referrals, you must take the information you have learned and absolutely begin applying it to your life right now...

"I'm so excited for you...I know that people are applying this system with incredible success. You can do it too! Will the payoff be immediate? Maybe, maybe not. Will you do everything perfectly the first time out? Probably not...

"The point is this: Begin! Begin right away! Also, the

ability to stick with it is a key point. If you get knocked down, get back up. If you get knocked down again, get back up again."

He closes his book with this: "My suggestion is to be persistent. Do the little things right, do them consistently, and realize that selling, networking, and life itself is simply a numbers game. Of course, when following proven techniques, the numbers seem to get a lot better.

"Learn the techniques, implement them beginning now, and be persistent, and you will network your everyday contacts into sales."

Thanks to Bob Burg for providing a tested, proven system for giving and getting referrals. You will find there are many outstanding business leaders who have generously shared their systems in the books they have written. Read and adopt those that will work for you and you will create a framework to support your business as it thrives and grows.

Lead Register

Date	Phone	Visit	Name/Address (if possible)	Source of Lead								
				Data Base	Yellow Pages	News Ad	Signs	Door Hangar	Referral	Name of Referral	Thank You	Other
[9]	[10]	[11]	[8]	[13]	[1]	[2]	[3]	[4]	[5]	[6]	[12]	[7]

The explanation for the bracketed numbers and instructions for completing this form follows.

We track leads to determine how our customers come to use our services.
This information will provide us with a measurement of our current marketing and advertising program, and help us decide how to wisely spend our advertising dollars in the future.

Step #1 Whenever a potential customer calls or visits our business, we say, "We are always trying to improve our service. May I ask how you heard about our company?" The response is recorded in the appropriate column on the Lead Register which is kept on the purple acrylic clipboard on the desk behind the front counter:

[1] Saw our ad in the Yellow Pages
[2] Saw our ad in the newspaper
[3] Saw the sign on the front of the building
[4] Found our flyer hanging on the door
[5] Was referred by someone else - If referred by someone else, ask if they would mind telling us who, so that we might thank that person: Record name of referring person [6]
[7] Other - indicate the source

Step #2 Ask the potential customer if they would like to be added to our database so that we could notify them in the future of any new products our special promotions. If yes: Record name and address [8]

Step #3 Fill in the date. [9]

Step #4 Check the phone box if the person called. [10]

Step #5 Check the visit box if the person came into the store. [11]

Step #6 After the potential customer hangs up or leaves the store, write thank you note to the party who provided the referral, if appropriate.

• Thank you note stationary is located on the second shelf, left side of the office supply cabinet.
• The name and address of the referring party may be located in the customer database. The most recent customer database printout is filed in the "Customer" binder on the top shelf of the bookcase behind the front counter. if the name and address is not in the database, check the phone book which is located on the second shelf of the bookcase behind the front counter.
• Stamps are located in the top right hand drawer of the desk.
• The message in the note is: "Today we had a delightful experience! Mr./Mrs./Ms. _____ called (dropped by) to inquire about our catering services. He (she) told us you had suggested our company. Thank you so much for referring us to your friends. We appreciate your continued support and we will continue to work to deserve your loyalty. Sincerely [sign your name]."
• After writing the thank you note, place a check in the las column of the Lead Register [12]

Sep #7 Add the name and address of the customer to the database (if the customer wants to be added). Instructions for this procedure are located on page 7 of the Customer Service section of the Procedure MAnual. After adding the name and address, place a check in the data box on the Lead Register. [13]

Sep #8 When all steps of the process have been completed, highlight the entire entry on the Lead Register. There is a yellow highlighter in the top drawer of the desk. This will be an instantly recognized indication that the process has been completed. [10]

10
Watch the Bottom Line

I have known, worked for and admired some most innovative, creative entrepreneurs. Great new ideas spring from them on a daily basis. I call them hot-air popcorn poppers because they take tiny kernels of ideas, expand them, and then blow them out to fall wherever they may. These creatively gifted visionaries hate detail work. They sometimes refer to accountants and financial analysts as "bean counters" with deference, because they recognize that they must have associates who are adept at monitoring the financial soundness of their businesses. Usually accounting and financial associates have degrees like Master of Business Administration (MBA) and titles like Chief Financial Officer (CFO) or Vice President of Finance and full-time responsibility for watching the bottom line.

Just like a diligent parent would become alarmed if a child suddenly developed a high temperature and would take measures to treat the child and restore health, these associates who monitor the financial state of a business will immediately call attention to indications that the business is "off its mark" and ensure that measures be taken to restore its health.

Unfortunately, not all businesses can afford to hire a CFO with an MBA, so a great many of them fail to provide for the systematic monitoring of financial health. It is very common for small businesses to outsource their accounting functions to bookkeepers who specialize in recording financial data but know little or nothing about financial analysis. Once a year, these businesses haul their bookkeeping records to their CPAs' offices for tax preparation. Occasionally, but not always, the CPAs counsel the owners about the financial fitness of their businesses. Under the circumstances, it is easy to understand why fifty percent of new businesses fail within their first year, and close to eighty percent by year five, if no one consistently analyzes financial fitness. Some business analysts believe that between sixty and eighty percent of small business failures result from financial problems.

Take, for instance, the story recounted by John Reith, vice president of Nations Bank in Prince Frederick, Maryland about one of his customers. The story appeared in an article by Linda Elkins entitled "Real Numbers Don't Deceive" in the March 1997 issue of *Nation's Business*. A successful electrical contractor decided to seize an opportunity to expand its operations into mechanical contracting. Unfortunately it bid and won contracts in this new endeavor without adequately researching and projecting its costs.

"They were a seat-of-the-pants business with no formal

accounting control to see on an interim basis how they were doing. They knew things were getting tight, but they didn't know why," said Reith. Because the firm had not adequately projected its costs, gross profit for mechanical engineering projects was disastrously thin. The owners were delighted that revenues were rapidly growing, but it wasn't until the company's accountant prepared tax returns after nearly a year that it became apparent the mechanical engineering function was "draining the business dry."

"But it was too late," said Reith. "Eventually the business had to close. Had they done their projections to begin with, they would have seen what was happening."

Small businesses do thrive, however, and frequently grow to be substantial enterprises. When several hundred of the top CEOs in America were surveyed for their perspective on what skills are necessary for the success of a business, their number one choice was financial management. Financial management skills included securing and maintaining capital, managing cash flow, containing expenditures, and collecting accounts in a timely way.

The Oregon Marketing and Business Initiative, funded by lottery dollars funneled through the Oregon Economic Development Department, consults with emerging technology and software companies. In an article in *The Oregonian*, August 3, 1997, John Rumler explained how these growing businesses open their financial books to consultants like Greg Hadley in order to identify immediate and long-term issues.

"An MBA graduate from Pepperdine University, Hadley completed postgraduate studies at Harvard Business School before buying 14 Southern California companies and retooling and selling them.

"A frequent lecturer at Stanford Graduate Business

School, Hadley says most of the young firms he helps are weak on financing and raising capital.

"With money tied up in inventory and accounts receivable, they struggle to meet payroll.

"Hadley says many don't see the danger in outgrowing their financing until too late.

"More than half of companies that file bankruptcy do so after their best revenue year, he says."

Build Value in Your Business

From the beginning of your venture, keep in mind that you want to build a business that has value. Dave Lakhani suggests, in the article "For What It's Worth," in the July 1997 issue of *Entrepreneur* magazine, "Establishing value in your business allows you to make sure that the thing you've worked on most of your life continues to pay you." Value is the amount that someone would pay to purchase your business on the open market. Part of that value is the cash flow that can be expected in the future, as well as current performance and net profits.

Says the article's author, Mark Hendricks, "Despite the value of value, many entrepreneurs aren't building it. In fact, many are decreasing the value of their companies, sometimes without even knowing it.

"Some entrepreneurs overpay themselves, taking too much value out of the business in the form of fringe benefits, perks and salaries for themselves and family members or friends. It's not unusual for entrepreneurs to manipulate these outlays to show lower profits for the corporation. But that's risky.

"'[The business owner] may not only be taking his profits, but he may also be taking the return on his investment capital,' warns Glen A. Larsen Jr., associate professor of finance at Indiana University. 'He may be harvesting his business without knowing it.' Instead, he recommends entrepreneurs pay themselves modest salaries, perhaps nothing at all in the beginning. 'Get the short term under control, make plans for the long term and start building value before taking anything out of [the business].'

"Another symptom of short-sightedness is the failure to keep accurate records. This is where most entrepreneurs make an easily correctable mistake very early on. To avoid this problem, recommends Don Taylor, 'Start off with the mind-set that you're going to sell [the business]. Pick a date when you are thinking about selling it. If no date comes to mind, pick ten years from now. Then, because you have done that, you know to start off with good books.'

"Good books include more than adequate financial records. They include manuals, handbooks and other documentation on the operational side of the company. This not only makes it more likely that a potential buyer will feel he or she can run the company, but it also aids internal management training, says Lakhani."

Ensure the Success of Your Venture

It is imperative that any business owner who wants to succeed must analyze financial data on a monthly, if not weekly or in some cases daily, basis. During the planning phase, you created the most sound financial projections possible based on the data you collected in your investigative process. Do the actual figures vary from projected figures? If so, by how much? What caused the variation? What adjustments must be made to marketing or operations in order to improve the financial situation if the variation is negative? Or, should adjustments be made to future projections if the variation is positive? Informed business decisions are dependent upon sound estimates of revenue, costs of sales and all other expenses.

Few start up businesses project profitability at the end of their first month; many do not project profitability by the end of the first year. However, businesses determined to succeed do project what their financial position will be at the end of each month and then monitor to see how closely actual figures conform to projections. In addition, they research industry standards and carefully monitor their own performance to see how closely it corresponds to those standards.

Prevent Misappropriation of Funds

Embezzlement is not a pleasant sounding word. It takes on a whole new, horrifying meaning if applied to your own business! Unfortunately, many small business owners find themselves hearing that word when they abdicate responsibility for the financial fitness of the business and turn over their record keeping function to an employee or an independent contractor. Not long ago I consulted with a business that had recently lost $60,000 through embezzlement activities of their in-house bookkeeper. The bookkeeper had been able to forge checks which she had written to a non-existent company. That non-existent company had a checking account which she had opened. The bookkeeper had been employed for several years before she began her illegal activities. During those years the owners had come to trust her, and they turned all accounting and financial activities over to her.

As I have expressed my dismay about the situation of this company to other small business owners, I have been overwhelmed with expressions of, "Oh, that happened to us too." Embezzlement is not a topic most owners want to discuss with their friends at Chamber of Commerce meetings, with their leads groups, or anywhere for that matter. So one cannot help but wonder how widespread this phenomenon is.

Priority One — Learn about Accounting and Financial Management

The way to protect yourself from embezzlement is to become knowledgeable about accounting and financial management, and to carefully monitor the condition of your business on a regular basis.

If you cannot afford to hire a CFO and do not have a strong background in accounting and finance, it is imperative that you make the development of skills in these areas a hot item on your action plan. Community colleges and Small Business Administration offices frequently offer courses in both subjects. The American Management Association offers correspondence courses in these disciplines. Business owners who plan to succeed will find a way to become knowledgeable in these areas and then they will monitor carefully the financial health of their businesses on a consistent basis.

There is a wonderful book written for the small business owner or CFO that I highly recommend because of its focus, clarity and ease of reading. In the preface to his book *Bottom Line Basics: Understand & Control Business Finances*, author Robert J. Low says, "My goal in writing this book has been to communicate that effective financial management in smaller businesses is both critical for success and involves much more than just accounting. By focusing on the practical uses and benefits of accounting, planning, and control, rather than the mechanics, I also hope to motivate non-financial managers to take a more active interest in financial management."

By the way, while I strongly advocate understanding financial management, I do not mean to suggest that the business owner needs to do the bookkeeping and accounting for the firm. Bookkeepers and accountants do the work they do because they are adept with numbers and enjoy working with them. In addition, they already own accounting software that allows them to work so quickly and efficiently that they may keep the books for many clients. Therefore, unless a business becomes large enough to merit the addition of a staff bookkeeper or an accounting department, it is often wise to outsource processing of the data that will provide the basis for financial decisions. Keep in mind, however, that outsourcing the processing of data is different than abdicating responsibility for examining and understanding the financial health of your business.

Impress Your Banker

Besides ensuring success and reducing the probability of the misallocation of your financial resources, there is another reason for learning to monitor the financial health of your business. Should there be a time when you want or need to secure additional financing to expand your business, bankers will be eager to talk with you if you can demonstrate to them that you know precisely how your business is doing and you can substantiate your request for funding with sound financial projections. Bankers field lots of requests for financing. Those that receive immediate and positive attention provide the information needed to make a decision in the most concise manner and are presented by a business owner who is intimately familiar with the financial condition of the business. Banks need assurance that the business owner is committed to the financial well-being of the business.

The Very Minimum

There are three basic accounting documents that should be produced on a regular, consistent basis, and which form the foundation of the financial data used to monitor a firm's fitness: the income statement, cash flow forecast and balance sheet. Through the advances of modern technology and computers, these three reports can be easily obtained in unreconciled, un-audited form on a daily basis if necessary.

The Cash Flow Forecast

For many businesses, a daily cash flow forecast is critical. It indicates whether there is money in the bank at the time of the report, as well as indicating anticipated daily inflows and outflows. Consequently, the cash-flow forecast is probably the most important financial management tool of all. It is possible to be profitable, but not to have cash for paying bills, especially for businesses that have sizable inventories or that do long-term contract work. It is critical to the survival of a business that cash-flow forecasting is done before start up to ensure that sufficient capitalization is provided.

To calculate cash flow for a given period, begin with the current bank balance. Add to that any anticipated income from all sources, and deduct any money that will go out during that time. The result is the cash that will be left at the end of the period. A negative balance indicates insufficient funds to meet obligations.

It is wise in preparing projections to overestimate expenses and underestimate revenue. Surplus cash can always be applied to debt, or used to grow the business. But insufficient cash predicts the demise of the venture.

The Income Statement

The income statement is sometimes referred to as a profit and loss statement. For a given period (a month or a year) it records revenue from sales and all expenses. Revenue less all the costs directly related to making, distributing and delivering the product or service of the business (cost of goods sold or variable expenses) provides a figure called gross profit. It is important to calculate the gross profit for each product or service provided, as well as the overall gross profit, in order to determine their individual value to the company. When one product or service consistently fails to produce a satisfactory level of gross profit, it may be necessary to raise the price or find a way to reduce the cost of goods sold. Or it may be necessary to remove that item from the product or service line. Failure to calculate the gross profit of each line item may have serious impact on the ability of a business to have a positive net profit.

Successful business owners diligently monitor overhead expenses as well as cost of sales expenses. They recognize that every expense is a reduction to their profitability, and they are in business for two reasons: to answer a customer need and to be profitable.

After gross profit is calculated, all other expenses of the business, including overhead, depreciation and taxes (indirect expenses) are deducted to reveal the net profit or loss for that period.

The Balance Sheet

The balance sheet provides an overall picture of the worth of a business at a given moment. All assets are listed. All liabilities are deducted from the assets. The difference is the value of the owner's equity in the business. This financial document is called a balance sheet because the total of the liabilities and owner's equity must equal the total assets of the company.

What Will You Do With the Information?

The information provided in these three basic financial documents will aid you in evaluating your original assumptions about the business, and in setting new goals for your business. If revenues are lower than anticipated, it may be necessary to come up with new marketing strategies or better customer retention systems. If expenses are high, how can you reduce them without jeopardizing the quality of your product or service? If cash inflow is slower than expected, it may be necessary to review accounts receivable collection procedures. Alvin Moscow, in *Managing,* says, "When you have mastered the numbers, you will no longer be reading numbers any more than you read words when reading books. You will be reading meanings."

Once you have developed proficiency at reading your actual financial statements, you can begin to play with new possibilities for your business. What if...you hire a new employee? What if...you place an ad in a publication? Every 'what if' question requires adjustments to your projections, both monthly and annual.

Many small business owners make changes to their businesses without first playing "what if" games to determine whether the changes will have a positive or negative impact on the overall well-being of the business. It is easy to become enthusiastic about advertising opportunities, new office equipment, all kinds of things which cost money but could enhance your business. The important step before buying anything is to project what consequence the purchase will have on your bottom line.

Expenses can be divided into two groups: strategic and non-strategic costs. Strategic costs are those expenses that are directly responsible for generating new business. Non-strategic costs are other expenses that are incurred in operating a business. In *Double Your Profits*, Bob Fifer says that his philosophy regarding these two categories of expenses is:

"1. We will outspend our competition for strategic costs, and spend this money in good times as well as bad.

"2. We will ruthlessly cut non-strategic costs to the bone.

"Outspending your competitors on strategic costs requires intelligence and judgment. You must distinguish those selling, marketing, and R&D expenditures that truly enhance the top and bottom lines from those that are wasteful and unlikely to pay off. There is no formula that anyone can give you to make that judgment; excellent management is eighty percent art and only twenty percent science. Applying that intelligence and judgment on an ongoing basis—distinguishing the truly worthwhile strategic expenditures from non-strategic costs—is what makes your job challenging and fun. In the end, however, you must be able to identify enough worthwhile strategic expenditures to ensure that you are outspending your competition for strategic costs by a considerable margin, as a percentage of revenues if not in absolute dollars: By spending more on truly strategic costs, you build your business.

"'Ruthlessly cutting non-strategic costs to the bone' requires an unwavering suspicion of every single non-strategic cost; assume it can be eliminated unless proven otherwise.

"Then why do so few businesses practice them (specific steps to cut costs) and achieve impressive levels of profitability? For one, because many managers don't truly care about profits. However, even many managers who do care about profits fail a second test: They lack the absolute commitment to profits, the tough, determined resolve to lead their organizations in a consistent way...Doubling your profits (or more) requires a leader who is focused, consistent, tough, and fair, and who is willing to stretch himself or herself and others in the organization to be different and better than the status quo or the average manager of this world...To say it another way, if you truly want much greater profits, and you're willing to make the tough decisions, then doubled profits are easy to achieve."

		Year 1		Year 3		Year 5		Year 10	
		Financial Projections							
Income		$	100,000	$	175,000	$	250,000	$	500,000
Cost of Goods Sold									
	Materials	$	45,000	$	78,750	$	112,500	$	225,000
	Packaging	$	1,000	$	1,750	$	2,500	$	5,000
	Freight	$	5,000	$	8,750	$	12,500	$	25,000
Gross Profit		$	49,000	$	85,750	$	122,500	$	245,000
Expenses									
	Advertising	$	4,000	$	4,500	$	4,500	$	8,000
	Auto Insurance	$	1,200	$	1,300	$	1,400	$	1,750
	Bank Charges	$	120	$	120	$	120	$	180
	Business Insurance	$	900	$	900	$	1,000	$	1,200
	Car & Truck	$	2,000	$	2,500	$	3,000	$	4,000
	Charitable Contributions	$	100	$	200	$	300	$	500
	Dues & Subscriptions	$	500	$	500	$	600	$	600
	Equipment Lease	$	1,500	$	1,500	$	1,500	$	2,000
	Health Insurance	$	1,800	$	1,800	$	1,800	$	3,600
	Legal & Accounting Fees	$	1,000	$	750	$	750	$	1,500
	Licenses	$	100	$	100	$	100	$	150
	Life Insurance	$	250	$	250	$	250	$	250
	Office Supplies	$	500	$	250	$	800	$	1,000
	Payroll	$	24,000	$	36,000	$	58,000	$	90,000
	Payroll Taxes	$	6,000	$	9,000	$	14,500	$	22,500
	Postage	$	3,200	$	2,800	$	3,200	$	4,000
	Maintenance & Repairs	$	500	$	700	$	800	$	1,200
	Rent	$	12,000	$	12,000	$	12,000	$	13,200
	Sales Promotion	$	500	$	500	$	500	$	1,000
	Samples	$	2,500	$	1,200	$	800	$	1,500
	Shop Display	$	1,000	$	500	$	500	$	800
	Telephone	$	1,200	$	1,200	$	1,200	$	1,320
	Utilities	$	3,600	$	3,600	$	3,600	$	4,000
	Worker's Comp	$	800	$	900	$	1,200	$	1,800
Total Expenses		$	68,470	$	82,170	$	111,220	$	164,250
Operating Profit		$	(19,470)	$	3,580	$	11,280	$	80,750
Other Income									
	Interest Income	$						$	2,000
Total Other Income		$		$		$		$	2,000
Other Expenses									
	Interest Expense	$	8,000	$	6,500	$	6,500	$	3,800
Total Other Expenses		$	8,000	$	6,500	$	6,500	$	3,800
Net Profit/Loss		$	(27,470)	$	(2,920)	$	4,780	$	78,950

11

Enlist Help

Successful business owners rarely achieve their goals without an extensive support system. Friends, family and associates who believe in their vision, abilities, and commitment lend moral support, participate in planning, and sometimes even dig in to help with the actual operations of the enterprise. Professional advisors, including attorneys, accountants, and consultants (e.g., marketing consultants, business development consultants, computer consultants) offer expertise in specific areas. Beyond these individuals, there are many systems that support the entrepreneur: books, magazines and tapes; Chambers of Commerce; industry associations; networking and leads groups; and community organizations. All have a place in the support system of the fledgling business owner.

Hiring Professional Expertise

Before you ever open the doors of your business you should select an attorney and an accountant to advise you on the legal and financial aspects of establishing your venture. If you do not know who to consult, call their professional associations for referrals to those practitioners who specialize in working with small business owners. Ask friends and associates for recommendations. Then interview at least two or three people in each profession. This is another due diligence process, so you will want to prepare a list of questions before your initial meeting. Most professionals will gladly provide a 15 minute informational interview. You want to be sure you select a practitioner with whom you have clear communication, who will support your endeavors, and who will be accessible to advise you as you grow your business.

Another professional who is increasingly found working with successful business owners is a professional coach. The coach is not a problem solver, a teacher, an advisor, or even an expert in a technical discipline; he or she is a sounding board, facilitator, counselor, awareness raiser whose sole purpose is to form an alliance with the client to forward the client's progress.

Business owners often feel very much alone in their role, uncertain about who to trust and confide in as they chart their course. They are not looking for someone else to direct them, but simply wish to consult a fresh mind, someone who brings no investment or position of his/her own, an outsider who is not involved with the venture.

A trained coach assists the owner in developing awareness, which is the product of focused attention, concentration and clarity. As the owner builds his business, the coach recognizes that the owner's potential is realized by optimizing his own individuality and uniqueness, never by molding him to another's opinion of what constitutes best practice. An independent coach reflects ideas, evokes solutions and supports their implementation in a way that few experts or advisors could ever do.

Coaches aren't just for start ups or small businesses. Companies like Merix Corp., a $160 million manufacturer of advanced electronic equipment, are developing relationships with coaches. Deborah Coleman left her high-ranking job at Apple Computer to take over as CEO of the newly formed Merix Corp. in 1994. Shortly after, she became acquainted with Kay Stepp, the former president and Chief Operations Officer (COO) of Portland General Electric Company. Stepp had decided her background and experience, coupled with her ability to model leadership, could benefit other business leaders, and had recently started a new venture, Executive Solutions, to act as a consultant to senior executives to help them create a "learning environment."

The two women created a coaching alliance that allowed Stepp to help Coleman eliminate anything that blocked her client from seeing, and solving, her company's problems. She accomplished this by being mentally present, listening, and asking questions about the assumptions her client had made. The process created focus and helped Coleman be clear about priorities.

Consultants specialize in one particular aspect of business, and they usually contract to provide their expertise for a specified duration of time or to accomplish a specific project. Since no one can be an expert on everything, hiring a consultant fills the gaps in the owner's knowledge base. Most small businesses cannot afford to hire a consultant during early developmental stages; they must rely on other support systems to get their businesses off the ground.

Books, Tapes, Magazines and the Internet

Groucho Marx once quipped, "Outside of a dog a book is man's best friend. Inside a dog it is too dark to read." Without any doubt, there is a sea of information available for the entrepreneur who is determined to build a successful business. And the sea grows bigger every year. Those books may become your best friends as you build your successful business.

I have referred in several chapters to some of the best books I have found most helpful, and there is a suggested reading list at the end of this book. Most of the books on that list are available in paperback, so building your own library should not break the bank. I recommend that business owners buy the books they find most helpful, because they can then write in the margins, attach sticky notes to the pages that have the most pertinent information for them, and re-read those that give them the greatest boost.

If you want to "test drive" books first, your library may be a great resource. In addition, trade books with other members of your support system. That cuts everybody's book expenses. You get to read everything, but only need to buy those books that you will want to keep as permanent parts of your reference library.

Someone once said, "The will to win is not nearly as important as the will to prepare to win." Write a goal for reading business books: "I will read one new business development book every month." Then create the strategies that you will implement to reach your goal. "I will read one half hour every night before bed," or "I will carry a book with me at all times to read while waiting for appointments, waiting for lunch to be served (assuming you dine alone!), waiting for the oil to be changed in my car." It is amazing how much time we waste in increments of two to ten minutes. Commit to using your waiting time to increase your knowledge about building a successful business. Finally, write action items for those strategies — and enjoy checking them off as your knowledge base expands.

Many books are now available on tape. This is my personal preference for learning and developing my knowledge base. The library has a limited assortment of business tapes, and I have listened to all of them at least once. I exchange tapes with friends who are as avid about learning as I am. And I buy many tapes. I never, never drive anywhere without a tape in my car. I listen to tapes when I walk or work out on the Stairmaster. Actually, as I write these words, two of my tape players are at the repair shop. I have literally worn them out!

Finally, be sure to read current periodicals, like *Inc.*, *Entrepreneur, Success, Fortune, Forbes, The Wall Street Journal, The Business Journal, Nation's Business* and others. Since you cannot operate your business in a vacuum, you will always be affected by what is happening in the economy (local, national and global) and in the business world. You will want to skim many publications to gain an overview, and then read those articles that have significance to your industry and your own business. When you read articles, be looking for trends and predictions. If you aren't adapting to the rapidly changing marketplace, you could find your business obsolete. Also, watch for strategies that you may want to incorporate into your business plan. Reinventing the wheel is costly and time-consuming. Adopting strategies that have been successful in other markets or other industries can be very cost effective, and sometimes can give you a strong timing advantage in your own industry.

It is also important to read periodicals written specifically for your industry. Subscriptions to some of these magazines and papers are included in association membership, which is addressed later in this chapter. Make a commitment to your business, your customers and your employees that you will read these industry publications so that you will always be on top of the latest developments.

The internet now provides instant access to a mind-boggling amount of information. The world is literally at our fingertips. Just one word of caution: it is possible to become involved in exploring the internet to the exclusion of other activities. Again, I recommend that you set a goal, such as "I will spend 30 minutes every day conducting research on the internet." Then devise some strategies to accomplish that goal — "I will set an alarm clock to notify me when 30 minutes have passed." Once again, create those Action Items and check them off when completed.

Associations

I suspect that within every industry an association has been formed to act as a clearinghouse for members, monitor the activities of the industry, watch for government policies that affect it, and provide information and other services to its members. There is a book at the library that lists every American association; what a great resource! Most associations also have web sites for easy access. Join an association that represents businesses in your industry. This is probably the easiest, most accessible source of information about issues that directly impact your business.

An association is there to inform and support its members. Most associations have annual conventions which provide an incredible opportunity to see and hear the best in the industry, as well as opportunities to form friendships and alliances with people whose businesses do the same work yours does. By sharing success stories (and sometimes failure stories) owners expand their knowledge base and may discover new goals and strategies for their businesses.

When you attend a convention, you have an opportunity to meet and develop relationships with industry leaders who often fill the roles of mentors to those just getting started. With the advice and encouragement of those who have achieved success, you may be able to accelerate the growth of your own business. It is a wise recipient of that kind of assistance who downstream gives the same kind of assistance to the next "new kid on the block."

It is incredibly powerful to be part of the fabric of your industry, and to know that you are not alone in your endeavors. Associations often publish journals or newsletters, and promote the books and tapes of members. Be sure you take advantage of those sources to find out how the best in the industry are doing so well.

Here is a tip about associations, or in fact, about any organizations you decide to join to improve the success of your business: be an active member. Don't throw your money away on memberships just for the sake of having your company listed in the roster. Other members know who attends meetings and takes an active role. Relationships are established with people we work with, like, and respect, not with names listed in a directory. Remember the suggestion in the networking section of Chapter Nine? Get involved in your association so that you maximize the value of your membership. The more you give, the more you will receive in return.

Professional Organizations

Join your local Chamber of Commerce. The Chamber cares about the success of its members, and so continually strives to present programs that will empower its members to prosper. The Chamber has a skeletal paid staff, and relies on the volunteer involvement of its members for direction and development of programs. The Chamber is incredibly responsive to its members. There are usually programs for large corporate members, and others for small businesses. Some Chambers have even developed very specific series such as high tech programs.

Attend every meeting that is appropriate for your business. Become an active member of a committee. You may be amazed to find that, for your small contribution of time and effort, you receive extensive benefits. Other members will become part of your support system, as you also become part of their network. You will receive referrals from people who know you, know your commitment to your values, and know the quality of your work. You may find opportunities to form alliances with other businesses in order to provide a complete package of products and services to a customer.

The Chamber is also a source of information about the local community and is delighted to assist you in getting what you need. If you need information about other communities, your local Chamber can connect you with those Chambers.

For many people, active membership in one organization is all they can handle during the early development stages of their business. But others may desire to get more involved in their communities. Is there another organization that you should join in order to fulfill your commitment?

Carefully consider your personal energy level and ability to handle multiple obligations, because one principle holds true for any group you decide to join — take an active role.

Leads Groups, Networking and Master Mind

Leads groups have sprung up in most communities. Some are nationwide organizations, with significant annual dues, strict attendance policies, and requirements for submitting leads to other members. At the other end of the continuum are grassroots groups with few regulations and sometimes no financial obligation. In between there are many variations on the theme.

Basically, leads groups gather for the purpose of exchanging marketing leads among members. One member may have a friend, relative, employee, customer, supplier, acquaintance, etc. who needs the product or service of a second member. To some degree a sense of obligation may be created in the mind of the recipient, and so he or she then keeps an eye open for a lead that can be passed back to the first member.

It is wise to keep a record of all leads that are provided by other members. Be sure to write a thank-you note for every lead you receive, and let the donor know the outcome. As with any other organization, tremendous benefits accrue to those members who participate actively. Other members appreciate their efforts, grow to respect them for their concern and generosity, and are happy to refer them to potential customers.

As I pointed out earlier, networking is vital to a company's success. As defined by cookie mogul Wally "Famous" Amos, networking is "making new friends and maintaining and growing existing relationships." It provides a connection to the wider world that most of us access through our families, friends, business associates, association members, personal service providers and other acquaintances. People who regularly keep in touch, and give as much as or more than they get, find that their occasional requests for assistance and advice are welcomed and accommodated.

I think it's important to repeat some of the major principles of successful networking. In order to strengthen network relationships, look for ways you can serve the people you know. List people with whom you would like to improve your relationship, and create at least one action item that you will take toward that end. Eliminate any relationships that are negative and damaging to you. Ask directly for assistance, and be receptive when it is offered. Always be ready and eager to give back.

Napoleon Hill spent his life researching the secrets of success. Some of the most celebrated and successful people of the twentieth century shared their insights with him during the course of his work, initially inspired by the industrialist Andrew Carnegie. Among the concepts he distilled from the collective experience of leaders like Edison, Bell, Ford, Wilson, Schwab, Morgan and Woolworth were these: that adversity can be turned into advantage; and that nurturing, harmonious relationships are vital to success. One of his practices, based on the concept of Master Mind, calls on the power of two or more people joined in a spirit of perfect harmony in order to attain a specific objective.

A Master Mind group consists of two to six persons who meet regularly in an atmosphere of trust and harmony for the purposes of providing mutual support and encouragement, and of believing for each other things which each, alone, may find difficult to embrace for him/herself. The group is established, not to solve members' problems, but to surrender to the Master Mind any problems, challenges, needs for healing, or positive desires. When such requests are fully and properly made, answers and solutions occur in a most amazing way, as a result of the energy created by the group.

Board of Advisors

Consider assembling a board of advisors, three or four professionals or business owners you respect and trust, possibly people you know from the organizations you have joined. Ask them to be your guests for breakfast or dinner once every six months to monitor your progress and give you feedback. Provide each advisor with a summary of your goals, strategies and outcomes. You may want to offer to return the favor. As you will soon find out, time is precious to business owners. But few would object to donating a few hours twice a year to help a friend build a successful business.

In the June 1997 *Success* magazine article, "The Self-Made Woman," Elaine Pofeldt tells the following story of Manhattanite Cynthia Ekberg Tsai, founding director of the biotechnology research company NuGene Technologies Inc., and general partner in the venture-capital fund MassTech Ventures.

"In the spring of 1995, Cynthia Ekberg Tsai came up with the idea of a lifetime. She would launch a huge health expo. Unlike the typical trade show, it would dazzle consumers with lively entertainment. She'd build a database of visitors.

"She teamed up with Anna Lynn Screpetis, 27, who was fresh out of the University of Texas with a master's degree in social work, and later, Bonnie Bothmann Wohlreich, 43, who had a marketing background.

"Working from Tsai's Fifth Avenue apartment, they created an advisory board, hired a public-relations company, and secured corporate sponsors, such as Panasonic.

"They're now getting ready to launch HealthExpo at the New York Coliseum in September. They expect to bring in $3.6 million in gross revenue this year."

Tsai didn't try to launch her idea alone. She partnered with two women whose skills and backgrounds complemented her own, and the three of them enlisted the assistance of a board of advisors, and hired professionals to render needed services. Tsai achieved her goal by creating an extensive support system.

12

You Can Transform
Your Dream Into Reality

She sat squirming, like any seven-year-old attending a meeting, while her Blue Bird leader made the announcement, "It's time for the annual Camp Fire candy sale, and I have great news!" That caught her attention, so she looked up to hear the announcement. "Any of you who can sell one hundred boxes of Camp Fire candy will earn a one-week scholarship to Camp Namanu." The girl's casual attention turned to rapt concentration.

It was shortly after the end of World War II, and while she lived in a nurturing, supportive family, she knew that money was tight. Her father was a salesman, her mother the church secretary. A week's tuition at camp for one of their three children would probably not be in the family budget.

The announcement was truly the light at the end of the tunnel, and now the leader proceeded to paint a vivid picture.

"At camp, you will sleep in a cabin with seven other girls and a counselor. When you get up in the morning, you'll dress in your navy blue shorts, white shirt, and red Camp Fire tie and go to the meadow for flag salute, songs and games. You will eat your meals in Raker Lodge with all the other campers, where there will be more singing, games and lots of fun. During the day you'll go to the craft cottages to learn how to weave on a loom, braid gimp and make pottery. There will be nature hikes in the forest. You will go to the swimming hole on the Sandy River. In the middle of the meadow is a pond with rowboats, which you can explore during your free time. You will write a letter to Squiggleboggle, the squirrel who lives in the magic tree in Sherwood Forest, and he will write back to you. And best of all, at night, gathered around the camp fire, you will sing songs, tell stories, toast marshmallows and eat s'mores (toasted marshmallows and Hershey bars sandwiched between graham crackers)."

That child was me! As I heard my Blue Bird leader talk about Camp Namanu, my imagination traveled there! I could see the meadow and the forest. I could hear the Sandy River rippling over stones, and the happy singing and laughter of the campers. I could smell the pine trees and the camp fire. And I could taste the s'mores!

As supportive as my parents were, can you imagine what they must have felt when after a long day at the office, they returned home to find one hundred boxes of peanut brittle stacked in the middle of the living room? There was no joy! But my young parents did two very wise things. First, they did not bail me out, but supported my dream. They could have said, "We didn't give you permission to order this candy. We're going to send it back to Camp Fire." They didn't do that. My father could have said, "The freight line will buy it, and the salesmen will give it to our customers." He didn't do that. My mother could have said, "I'll take it to the church. People there will buy it." She didn't do that. Instead, they said to me, "You have a dream. You can sell this candy."

The second thing they did was create the steps I needed to take to transform my dream into reality. My father said, "We're going to go down to the basement to write a little sales speech for you." Now I have done lots of right things in my life, and I have done my share of wrong things. But one of the "rightest" things I ever did was to choose a father who was in sales! My father continued, "You're going to memorize that speech, and after school, while it's still light, you're going to go into the immediate neighborhood to sell your candy. You're going to knock on every door, give your little speech, and sell your candy. After dinner, I'm going to take you to other neighborhoods. I'll be with you, but you are going to knock on the door, give your little speech, and sell your candy." My mother said, "On Saturday, when I don't have to work, we're going to take a card table to the neighborhood grocery store. You're going to give your little speech to everyone who goes into the store, and you're going to sell your candy."

No kid at Camp Namanu that summer enjoyed her week more than I did. Because I earned it! My parents in their youthful wisdom had not robbed me of the self-esteem building opportunity to sell the candy myself. My Blue Bird leader had created the vision, my parents had supported my belief in my ability to reach that vision and produced the steps I needed to take to transform my dream to reality, and I eagerly took those steps.

At a very tender and formative age my parents helped me develop skills that would empower me all my life. Whenever I have dreamed of reaching a goal, I have outlined the path I would need to take to get there, and then created the action steps I would take. Have I always reached my goals? Heavens no! When I was eight, I wanted desperately to be a Junior Rose Festival princess. I was selected as my grade school's candidate. My father and I wrote a little speech, which I practiced and delivered perfectly. My mother made me a delightful mauve organza dress — for an avowed tomboy, I looked darned cute the night of the competition. But I didn't win. Was I destroyed? Never! At eight years old, I was thrilled to shed the dress, don my overalls and head back to climbing trees and chasing garter snakes!

When I was a junior I competed to be my high school's representative to Oregon Girl's State. I was ecstatic when selected. At Girl's State I desperately wanted to be elected Secretary of State. I campaigned diligently, but lost to a brilliant girl whose acquaintance I was pleased to have made. Did it set me back? Momentarily, perhaps, but I was soon steeped in the pursuit of some new goal.

When I bought my first business, a franchise, I thought I would be fantastically successful. Because I truly believe that attitude makes an enormous difference in what we achieve, I tackled building my business with enthusiasm and high energy. At the convention I attended before I had even been in business for a year, I was awarded the first ever Positive Thinkers Award, "in recognition of your positive mental attitude. This attitude is reflected in the way you approach your work, your life and in the way you interact with people." Two years later I abandoned my franchise when I realized that although I was working diligently and generating substantial revenues, I would never earn a net income commensurate with the time and energy I was committing to the business. Like Thomas Edison, I had just successfully discovered one way that I would not build a financially rewarding business.

Undeterred, I went on to open a second business in the same industry, but outside the geographical limits of the non-compete agreement I had with the franchiser. Drawing on what I had learned from my prior lack of success, I made a number of changes, and this time the business was very successful.

The point is, go after your dream. Begin by clearly envisioning exactly what you want to achieve in the short and long term. Believe that you can achieve your dream. Then create the steps you will need to take to transform your dream into reality.

The information provided in this book is designed to give you some very basic tools for building a successful business. Remember, there is no single book that can give you all the answers. There is no one great guru who can tell you what you need to do. You have within yourself the power to create a successful business. However, there are sound, basic business principles that underlie every successful endeavor. As a business owner, it is your responsibility to acquire and use the tools of ownership: visualizing, planning, developing systems, getting help from advisors and coaches, and measuring and monitoring results.

And when you hit a bump in the road, step back to assess what you can learn, try another strategy, and then resume your march toward success! Remind yourself of Henry Ford's words, "If you believe you can or cannot, you are 100 percent correct."

Business Owner's Basic Reading List

(Books That Will Empower You to Transform Your Dream Into Reality)

Bottom Line Basics, Understand & Control Business Finances, Robert J. Low, Paperback book

The E-Myth Revisited: Why Most Small Businesses Don't Work and What to Do About It, Michael E. Gerber Paperback book

Endless Referrals, Bob Burg, Paperback book

Guerrilla Selling : Unconventional Weapons and Tactics for Increasing Your Sales, Bill Gallagher, Orvel Ray Wilson, Jay Conrad Levinson, Paperback book and audio cassette

Beware the Naked Man Who Offers You His Shirt: Do What You Love, Love What You Do and Deliver More Than You Promise, Harvey Mackay, Paperback book

Dig Your Well Before You're Thirsty: The Only Networking Book You'll Ever Need, Harvey Mackay, Paperback book

How to Build a Network of Power Relationships, Harvey Mackay, Audio Cassette

Swim With the Sharks Without Being Eaten Alive: Outsell, Outmanage, Outmotivate, and

Outnegotiate Your Competition, Harvey Mackay, Paperback book

Sharkproof, by Harvey Mackay, Audio Cassette

Double Your Profits in 6 Months or Less, Bob Fifer, Paperback book

Customer Loyalty, How to Earn It, How to Keep It, Jill Griffin, Hardcover book

301 Great Customer Service Ideas : From America's Most Innovative Small Companies (301 Series), Nancy Artz

(Editor), Harvey MacKay , Paperback book

What's Luck Got to Do With It?: Twelve Entrepreneurs Reveal the Secrets Behind Their Success, Gregory K. Ericksen (Editor), Ernst, Young, Paperback book

The Portable MBA in Entrepreneurship (2nd Ed) (Portable MBA Series William D. Bygrave\, Hardcover book

For Entrepreneurs Only : Success Strategies for Anyone Starting or Growing a Business, Wilson L. Harrell, Hardcover book

Essentials of Entrepreneurship and Small Business Management, Thomas W. Zimmerer, Norman M. Scarborough, Paperback book

The Balanced Scorecard : Translating Strategy into Action, Robert S. Kaplan, David P. NortonList, Hardcover book

The Psychology of Selling, Brian Tracy, Paperback book and audio cassette (hard to find)

INDEX

Accountants 171, 176, 185-186
Accounting 121,135. 153. 160. 171. 173, 177-178
Action Items 129, 138, 140-144, 146, 153, 189
American Management Association 107, 177
Attorneys 57, 185-186
Balance Sheet 106-107, 179, 181
Bankers 99, 178
Benchmarks 144-147
Board of Advisors 57, 195-196
Bookkeeper 176, 177
Books 185, 188
Brainstorming 118, 145
Cash Flow Forecast 120, 174, 179-180
CFO 171, 172
Chamber of Commerce 107, 135, 177, 185, 192
Computers 160-161
Consultants 157, 158, 185, 187
Conventions 158, 191
Corporate Downsizing 15, 16
Cost of Goods Sold 180
CPA 57, 70, 172
Customer Service 57, 149-152, 156, 159
Customer Surveys 150, 156-158
Customers 91, 150-152
Due diligence 56 141, 186
Embezzlement 176-177
Employee Training 154
Expenses 182
Feasibility 31, 51-64
Finance 103, 147
Financial; Management 107, 173, 177
Financial Projections 120, 136, 173
Financial Statements 58, 181
Franchises 15, 16-18, 48
Goals 26-29, 30, 96, 114, 117-118, 127, 145, 185, 188

Gross Profit 180
Home-based Business 15
Income Statemnt 179-180
Industry Associations 158, 185, 190-191
Internet 168, 188, 199
Inventories 174
Investment Capital 106, 174
Lead Groups 185, 193-195
Marketing 91, 175
Master Mind 194-195
Mission Staement 57, 87-91
Network (Multi-level) Marketing 15, 17-18
Networking 161-166, 185, 193-195
Operations 103, 175
Owner's Equity 174-175
Periodicals 64, 135, 185, 189-190
Procedural Manuals 154, 159
Procedures 150, 154-156
Professional Advisors 185
Professional Coach 186-187
Profits 174, 182-183
Revenues 180, 181
Risk 65-79, 106
Rules 154-156
Sales & Marketing 103
Small Business Administration 177
Strategic Costs 133, 182-183
Strategic Plan 95-126, 128, 136, 137, 138, 139
Strategic Time 133
Systems 145, 147, 153-154, 160-161, 166
Tapes 185, 189
360 Feedback 33-34, 59
Time Management 132-135
Undercapitalization 56
Values 13, 21, 23-26, 30, 86
Vision 18, 57, 81-87, 112, 113

Joan Hartley is available for speaker, keynote addresses, seminars, and other special presentations. To find out how to schedule her for your organization's most important event(s), call (503) 292-6269

To order additional copies of

The Business Owner's
Basic Toolkit for Success

Contact: BookPartners, Inc.
P.O. Box 922
Wilsonville, Oregon 97070
Phone: (503) 682-8684
Phone: 1-800-895-7323
Fax: (503) 682-8684
E-mail: bpbooks@teleport.com